Mu Shiying

RAS CHINA in SHANGHAI

RAS China in Shanghai series

In 1857 a small group of British and Americans seeking intellectual engagement in a city dedicated to commerce established the Shanghai Literary and Scientific Society. Within a year the organisation was granted affiliation with the Royal Asiatic Society of Great Britain and Ireland in London and the North China Branch of the Royal Asiatic Society was born. The Society was re-convened in Shanghai in 2007.

The RAS China in Shanghai series of China Monographs, published in association with Hong Kong University Press, is designed to reflect the vibrancy as well as the wide research interests and contacts of the Society and to provide a forum for its members and associates to publish their research interests.

Series Editor: Paul French

Other titles in the RAS China in Shanghai series:

Knowledge Is Pleasure: Florence Ayscough in Shanghai
Lindsay Shen

Lao She in London
Anne Witchard

The Happy Hsiungs: Performing China and the Struggle for Modernity
Diana Yeh

Mu Shiying

China's Lost Modernist

New Translations and an Appreciation
by Andrew David Field

香港大學出版社
HONG KONG UNIVERSITY PRESS

Hong Kong University Press
The University of Hong Kong
Pokfulam Road
Hong Kong
www.hkupress.org

Permission to reproduce Randolph Trumbull's translation of 'Five in a Nightclub' courtesy of *Renditions*, a publication of the Research Centre for Translation of The Chinese University of Hong Kong.

ISBN 978-988-8208-14-2

British Library Cataloguing-in-Publication Data
A catalogue record for this book is available from the British Library.

Digitally printed

Contents

Illustrations

Acknowledgements

I would like to begin by thanking David Der-wei Wang for introducing me to the enigmatic figure of Mu Shiying. During a graduate seminar on modern Chinese literature, held at Columbia University in 1994, Professor Wang exposed us to the stories of Mu Shiying and other 'Shanghai modernists'. Over the years, in addition to counselling me on my doctoral dissertation on China's Jazz Age, which eventually became the subject of my book, *Shanghai's Dancing World*, Professor Wang always encouraged me to pursue a writing project on Mu Shiying.

Leo Ou-fan Lee's exemplary work on Mu Shiying and other 'Shanghai modernist' writers brought them into the limelight of Western academic scholarship during the 1990s, culminating in his masterwork, *Shanghai Modern: The Flowering of a New Urban Culture in China, 1930–1945*. Professor Lee was extremely supportive during the research for my dissertation and first book, and he has indirectly influenced the making of this book as well. In addition, I must also acknowledge the wonderful work of Shu-mei Shih, whose book *The Lure of the Modern* represents the best scholarship in the English language on Mu and other Shanghai modernists. In researching my own essay on Mu's life and works, I have drawn on the works of these scholars—I am indebted to them, even if I have taken some liberties with my own interpretations of Mu's life and works.

How this book came together is another story. Knowing of my interest in Mu Shiying and the period in which he lived, Paul French asked me if I would like to publish a short volume about the author, which would include translations of some of his stories as well as a lengthy appreciation of his life, times and works. Hong Yu served as co-translator throughout the process of translating these stories. Mu's writings posed many linguistic and semantic challenges, but working together we were able to surmount them and provide translations that are intended to reflect the spirit and meaning of his original writings, while also making them accessible and engaging to the English reader.

We leave it to the reader to judge the efficacy of these translations. Our goal has been to cleave as closely as possible to the rhythm, style and meaning of his stories, which are not always easy to process in their original language, let alone in translation. Thus, my thanks go to Paul French for providing me with this wonderful opportunity to bring Mu to the world, and to Hong Yu for her patience and dedication to the task of co-translation. A special thanks goes to the Royal Asiatic Society in Shanghai for supporting and helping to fund the making of this book. Another word of thanks goes to Randolph Trumbull for his own outstanding translation of 'Five in a Nightclub', and to the journal *Renditions* for kindly allowing us to publish it in this volume. Finally, I would like to thank Michael Duckworth at Hong Kong University Press for agreeing to publish this volume.

—Andrew David Field

A Chinese Perspective on Mu Shiying: A Note from the Co-Translator

The first time I read Mu Shiying, I was stunned and amazed by his story 'Shanghai Fox-trot'. During the process of co-translating several of his works for this book, I felt as if I were in a glider flying low across the landscape of a Shanghai fashioned by Mu's words. From his writings about urban life, within the political context of the times, one marvels at the flexibility, charm and freedom of his prose. Whether one examines Mu Shiying's deliberate choice of florid language and the experimental style of his early writings, or the avant-garde qualities of his later writings on metropolitan life, even today one can still admire them and see them as being on the cutting edge of Chinese language and literature.

The modernity of his works also lies in their contents, particularly in the fresh and unique ways that he explores the space of the modern metropolis and the ongoing tug of war between men and women within that space. His female characters, who make a living by brazenly embracing men in public arenas, have love lives that are daring and progressive even by today's standards. And one is still shocked by how he portrays women such as 'Craven A', focusing as he does on the erotic landscape of their bodies.

Mu Shiying had the qualities of what we would today call 'modernity' within the field of contemporary arts. He possessed the modern style of the artists of 1920s Paris. He and Walter Benjamin (the early twentieth-century German Jewish literary critic and philosopher) both used the literature of the senses to study the modern urban condition. What is even more compelling is that Mu Shiying himself participated fully in modern urban culture, experiencing and consuming all of the pleasures of the modern Asian metropolis. Like the American artist Andy Warhol, who embraced the consumer's paradise of 1960s New York, Mu threw himself onto the stage of contemporary urban life in 1930s Shanghai and made it the subject of his art. Certainly, there must be some deep aesthetic reflections that can come of studying how artists from different generations have drawn from and interacted with the exotic cultural environments and consumption spaces of different metropolises in modern times.

From this perspective, one can see that Mu was among the first generation of worldly cosmopolitans in China. As a youthful literary genius, he placed himself firmly within the camp of left-wing writers. Yet after his debut (with 'Poles Apart'), he genuinely embraced the attitude of an urban literatus and became embroiled in the spaces and cultures of contemporary urban life. Only then, with the publications of stories such as those we have translated for this book, did he truly emerge as a modernist Chinese writer. He bravely and independently carved out a lifestyle and a literary style that earned him a prominent place within the pantheon of Shanghai modernists. Withstanding the pressures of more traditional Chinese cultural practices, he stubbornly carved out his own literary career by celebrating his passions for sultry dancers and people from all walks of life, while portraying the ins and outs of urban nightlife and critically examining the treacherous terrain of youthful love.

From Mu's works, we can see how modernist literature sprang forth like a 'flower of evil' from the harsh soil of city life in 1930s Shanghai, within the context of class politics, in which Chinese writers had to choose sides. His struggle for artistic autonomy reflects that of many modern and contemporary artists and intellectuals in China to find their own voices and places amid the ever-changing landscape of urban modernity. Severed from ties to traditional forms of Chinese culture, Mu and others of his age and beyond have continually been caught up in a quest to define their identity as artists and as Chinese. The striving of these artists from the 1930s is a continual source of inspiration to subsequent generations of intellectuals caught up in similar struggles in today's China.

From the wartime era of the 1930s and 40s up to the present day, the problems associated with China's modernization have comprised a large theme of discussion for Chinese intellectuals. In the late 1920s, these intellectuals faced the crisis of their own definition as such. By the time of Mu Shiying in the 1930s, these writers had coalesced into groups of like-minded people within the Chinese literary world. While in Hong Kong, Mu Shiying's friendship with the artist Wang Shaoling (1909–1989) and his explorations of the film industry and film language (he wrote for and directed films though they were never screened) are a reminder to us: during that era, artists such as Mu were striving to embrace many different forms of art (film, dance, visual arts, literature) and use them to further their artistic goals. These were the true modern artists.

Mu Shiying was a controversial artist in his time. He bottled himself up in his own writings and always played himself, memorializing and immortalizing himself in his prose. This project of translation is thus a resurrection of a unique artist long since forgotten by the bulk of the Chinese reading public, and barely known by those outside of China during his lifetime.

—Hong Yu, Shanghai 2013
(translated from Chinese by Andrew David Field)

Mu Shiying: An Appreciation of His Life, Times and Works

During the 1930s, Shanghai was infamous for its outrageous blend of Chinese and Western modernities. Tall buildings such as the famed Park Hotel stuck out against a low-lying backdrop of *lilong* neighbourhoods composed of neat rows of identical brick lane-houses. Multi-storey Western-style department stores pushed themselves out prominently and proudly onto Nanjing Road, thrusting modern commercial practices into a field of commerce hitherto dominated by narrow and colourful outdoor street markets, small-scale retail stores and pawnshops. Deco-style cinemas decorated with gigantic posters of the latest Hollywood film stars competed for the public's attention with Chinese opera houses and 'storytelling halls' emblazoned with the names of famous Chinese opera singers and courtesans. On the streets, brightly coloured cars vied with rickshaws. At night, the city skyline came ablaze with neon signs advertising restaurants and nightclubs, and the sounds of jazz poured out of the revolving doors leading to the city's numerous ballroom dance halls. Such a heady concoction of contradictory sensations, stimulations and experiences produced a fertile literary field, one that in the sphere of Chinese *belles lettres* was as influential as Paris and New York were to their counterparts in the West.

Among the many Chinese writers who set forth, pen in hand, to document the life of the city during that era was a young man with the surname Mu and the given name Shiying. Hailing from the town of Cixi, near Ningbo in Zhejiang Province, Mu moved to Shanghai at the dawn of the 1930s to attend Aurora University. His father, a banker and gold speculator, had died of depression and exhaustion after losing his fortune. Rather than following in the glorious footsteps of the family patriarch, Mu Shiying instead threw himself into the world of letters and earned a modest living with his pen while sampling the delights and diversions of the city's varied consumption and entertainment venues. Soon after planting himself in the fertile soil of modern urban life, the budding writer took the city's literary world by storm, launching a meteoric career in letters at the tender age of seventeen. His earliest stories attracted the attention of Shi Zhecun, who edited one of the most influential literary journals in Shanghai, *Les Contemporains* (*Xiandai*). Mu became a close companion and protégé of Shi and other modernist writers such as Liu Na'ou and Dai Wangshu. He would soon emerge as the leading exemplar of Shanghai's own unique version of literary modernism. Ten years later, after taking a top post in a pro-Japanese journal, the handsome young author would fall to an assassin's bullets while riding in a rickshaw on his way to work. Bleeding to death on the way to the hospital, Mu ended his life as one of countless victims of the underground war between 'collaborators' and 'resistors' that was taking place during the Japanese military occupation of Shanghai.[1]

During his short lifespan, Mu Shiying produced a prodigious outpouring of short stories, novels and essays.[2] While loosely associated with the group of writers known collectively as the 'new

在达特安邮船上，送戴望舒赴法留学
自左至右，施蛰存、穆时英、戴望舒、杜衡（1932年10月8日）

Figure 1
Left to right: Shi Zhecun, Mu Shiying, Dai Wangshu and Du Heng.
Source: Yan Jiayan et al., *The Collected Works of Mu Shiying* (*Mu Shiying quanji*).

sensationalists' (*xin ganjue pai*), who sought to capture in words the sensations of modern urban life, he would maintain a fierce sense of independence from all literary trends and sects. Many of his literary productions, particularly his earlier ones, endeavoured to depict the pace, speed and spirit of the city in its many guises, and to describe the various moods and experiences of its diverse denizens as they coped with the onslaught of the vigorous interwar phase of Western-style capitalist modernity. Mu wrote critically about the experiences of his fellow Chinese countrymen living under the yoke of 'semi-colonialism', but he did so without falling prey to the ideological fervour that had gripped many other young Chinese writers of the age.

Mu came of age in interesting times. In 1931, the army of Imperial Japan attacked and occupied Manchuria, eventually creating a puppet state headed by the last Manchu emperor, Puyi. Starting on 28 January 1932 and for several weeks thereafter, Shanghai endured a brief but devastating war between Japanese and Chinese forces in the northern sector of Zhabei, which was utterly demolished. This conflict involved the first extensive aerial bombing campaign against a largely civilian population—Chinese refugees fled into the two foreign settlements by the thousands—and set a dire tone for the much larger war to come.[3] During this period of heightened nationalism and patriotic calls to 'save the nation' (*jiuguo*), Mu remained largely aloof of ideological concerns, choosing to dwell in his own inventive and imaginary world of literary experimentation as he carved out his unique writing career. For his stance of cultivated neutrality towards the 'Japanese menace', his tendency to indulge in the pleasures of the metropolis both in reality and in fiction, and his intentional distancing from the ideologies of the age, Mu would earn the anger and contempt of other writers who dedicated themselves to the monumental

Figure 2
Mu Shiying and his wife, Qiu Peipei. Source: Yan Jiayan et al., *The Collected Works of Mu Shiying* (*Mu Shiying quanji*).

task of 'saving the nation' in a tragic age of political fragmentation, foreign imperialism, invasion and war. He would even have to endure a scathing personal critique by Lu Xun, then the most powerful voice in the Chinese world of letters, who castigated him for choosing to write stories about the urban petty bourgeoisie in an age of national crisis.[4]

Several years later, while he was eking out a stark existence in Hong Kong with his wife Qiu Peipei, economic considerations as well as an unhealthy dose of idealism compelled Mu to take a job with the newly formed 'peace movement' under the leadership of Wang Jingwei and collaborate with the national enemy, Japan. This led to his assassination in June 1940. Owing to his untimely death and to the subsequent decades of revolutionary politics that would canonize those writers who focused on the desperate plight of the rural poor rather than on the colourful lifestyles of the urban middle classes, Mu's literary oeuvre would be submerged for decades, only to re-emerge in China in the 1980s. Another possible interpretation is that it took that long for the rest of the country to catch up with him. Indeed, there are hints in his writings that suggest that Mu was a very forward-looking thinker, that he had an uncanny predictive sense of what sort of city Shanghai would eventually become, half a century or more after his death.

Since his revival in the Chinese literary and intellectual landscape beginning in the 1980s, Mu has once again taken on legendary status as a 'literary comet', who showered such bright sparks upon Shanghai's glittering world of Chinese *belles lettres* and *bon mots* that he lit up the entire city in neon words.[5] In the process, he exposed the dark underbelly of a city notoriously ridden with gangsters, opium dens and prostitution, while also capturing the unbridled hedonism and boundless energy of the metropolis in its heyday. Mu's works probed the life of the city with a highly

Figure 3

Mu Shiying. Source: Yan Jiayan et al., *The Collected Works of Mu Shiying* (*Mu Shiying quanji*).

inventive and rhythmic language that owed as much to the influence of jazz music and the fox-trot as it did to the chants of the dock workers who plied the Bund.

Since the 're-discovery' of Mu in the 1980s by literary scholars in China, most notably Yan Jiayan, his works and those by other like-minded writers have been subject to many republications, compilations and critical analyses.[6] One such compilation, *Selected Stories from the Shanghai School*, serves as a good example. The volume contains works by over a dozen modernist Shanghai writers from the 1930s and 1940s.[7] Among the writers chosen for inclusion are Liu Na'ou and Shi Zhecun, Du Heng, Ye Lingfeng, Zhang Ailing, Xu Xu and others. Some of these writers—notably Liu Na'ou, Shi Zhecun and Du Heng—were Mu's compatriots, nighttime companions and literary mentors, though in the end he outshone them all with the sheer brilliance of his prose. Even Zhang Ailing (Eileen Chang), who would influence generations of Chinese writers with her own unique literary style, claimed to have been influenced by Mu.[8] The editors of this particular collection included five works by Mu, which might serve as his 'best of' list: 'Poles Apart', 'Platinum Statue of a Female Nude', 'Shanghai Fox-trot', 'The Man Who Was Treated as a Plaything', and 'Five in a Nightclub'. As the editor notes in the preface to this compilation, 'Mu Shiying was most adept at capturing the moods of the various types of urbanites who were jaded from the pressures of metropolitan life, and he cleverly employed a mixture of realism and modernism in an artistic flourish all his own, revealing the stark separation between the lives of the rich and the poor, with "Shanghai Fox-trot" being his most exemplary work.'[9]

Indeed, today, Mu's most famous work is probably the story 'Shanghai Fox-trot'. Loosely constructed as a series of montage-like scenes, this story follows several characters on a nocturnal journey into the city's finest ballrooms and hotels, but also onto its most dangerous construction sites and its darkest alleyways. One of the six stories featured in this book, 'Shanghai Fox-trot' best exemplifies Mu's distinctive experimental approach to writing, which drew upon various strains and styles of modernist literature then being explored in the West and in neighbouring Japan. Like his friend Liu Na'ou, Mu would cite French writer Paul Morand and Japanese writer Yokomitsu Riichi as two of his big influences (in 1928, Liu Na'ou had brought works by Riichi and other Japanese modernists over from Tokyo and had them translated into Chinese through a publishing house that he established).[10] Rather than conforming to the lines of a firmly fixed plot, the story unfolds in a pastiche of visions and sensations, whose flights of fancy, unfixed point-of-view and stream-of-consciousness passages might be compared to those by the American writer Thomas Pynchon, an author whom Mu would have certainly appreciated had he lived to read his works. One might also find affinities between Mu's stream-of-consciousness passages and interior monologues in the works of James Joyce, who undoubtedly was an influence on Mu, even if indirectly. 'Shanghai Fox-trot' also reveals Mu's strong interest in the new medium of film, which continued to influence many of his literary works in terms of both content and form.[11] Most of all, Mu's story 'Shanghai Fox-trot' is ablaze with the devil-may-care sexuality of men and women hell-bent on maximizing their carnal pleasures in the metropolis.

'Shanghai Fox-trot' also contains traces of his early interest in the lives of both the urban and lumpen proletariats. Yet unlike his early work 'Poles Apart', which follows the tale of a young, uneducated rural roustabout who is inadvertently thrust into the life of the big city, in 'Shanghai Fox-trot' the city's poor serve mainly as background figures for his study of the wealthier classes. They are the people who pay for the pleasures of the wealthy and privileged with their bodies and their lives. In one scene, a construction worker dies in an accident while working on a building that is slated to become a hotel, restaurant and dance hall. In another scene, a writer, clearly based on the author himself, encounters a woman who leads him into an alley to read a letter, only to prostitute her own daughter-in-law to him so that they can afford to eat a meal. These brief portrayals of the down-and-out reflected the grim realities of the majority of those who eked out a living in the city during the interwar era. For these people, life in the big city was a daily struggle for survival. For those with means, on the other hand, Shanghai served as a dreamy playground, a phantasmagoria filled with ephemeral and elusive pleasures and amusements—yet one in which the nightmarish reality of stock market crashes, crushing poverty, civil strife and brewing world wars always followed in hot pursuit. This *carpe diem* mentality was par for the course in a city whose bourgeoisie was in constant fear of being kidnapped, assassinated or simply held to extortion by the notorious Green Gang, which enjoyed a precarious alliance with the Nationalist government under Chiang Kai-shek after helping in 1927 to rid the city of Communists through a violent purge on April 12.[12]

Ultimately, Mu's focus on the hedonistic lifestyles of the more worldly and well-educated Chinese urbanites of Shanghai reflects his own social standing as well as his age at the time of writing. As mentioned earlier, Mu came from a privileged family background, the scion of a wealthy banker and gold speculator. Born on the brink of the new Republican era, Mu was well educated as a young boy and steeped himself early on in modern world literature, eschewing if not rejecting the more classical Chinese education that even then was available. Despite the turn in his family fortunes in the 1920s, Mu completed his education in Shanghai's prestigious Université l'Aurore (or, Aurora University), a Jesuit school founded in 1903. Even as his father's estate sank into desuetude following his reckless speculations, Mu still retained the airs of a pampered and elite young man. Images preserved of Mu as well as accounts of him by friends and associates all suggest that he was a dashing beau. His angular features, slicked-back hair and Western-style clothing suggest a raffish and refined elegance. Mu was certainly a debonair man-about-town, perhaps even a dandy. As attested by his companions and by his own letters and works of fiction, he frequented dance halls and nightclubs. These spaces of a Westernized urban modernity became the loci or at least the touch-points of many of his short stories. Judging from records left by him and others, Mu was a fantastic and avid dancer, who often danced and drank the night away. He chased girls and was chased by them in turn. His own dubious experiences with the city and its women became the fodder for some of his best works.

Born at the dawn of Republican China, which had violently displaced the outdated imperial system in 1912, Mu came of age during the 1920s. Following on the heels of the May Fourth Movement of 1919, this was a period of watershed changes in the lives and outlooks of a new generation of young, educated, urbanized Chinese, who strove to cast off the 'feudal yoke' of China's great tradition and venture forth into a new and freer world of unfettered human relations, loosely modelled on their perceptions and misperceptions of the West.[13] The contrast between a city like Shanghai and most of rural China, still mired in its ancient customs, superstitions and folkways, could not have been starker. Mu's early effort, in the tale 'Poles Apart', to depict the dubious transformation of a naive but vigorous 'country bumpkin' into a streetwise urbanite as well as his constant references to country life in his later works suggest that he was both familiar with and sympathetic to those who chose to remain in a rural setting rather than migrate to the big city. Mu himself taught for a spell at a rural elementary school. Nevertheless, big city life was clearly his own preference; even during his stint as a country teacher, he would spend his weekends in the dance halls of Shanghai. One of the attractive lures of the metropolis was the presence of numerous young, willing and available women. Unlike their rural counterparts, the women of Shanghai, at least in Mu's fictional works if not in reality, were gorgeous, mysterious, modern and, above all, sexually active.

The stories that we offer in translated form in this book are drawn from his second book of collected short stories, *Public Cemetery*, which was published in 1933. City women and their sexual promiscuity was a central and abiding issue in Mu's early works, which nearly always featured a young male narrator who was infatuated—whether briefly or at length—with a young woman who spent her time in the city's cabarets. As Mu writes in the preface to this collection, these stories were written with a similar design in mind:[14]

> At that time I simply wanted to describe something about the pierrot who had fallen in life and sunk into poverty. In my society there are those who have been crushed flat by life and those who have been squeezed out by life, but by no means do they necessarily, or let us say inevitably, show the face of opposition, tragic anger, or enmity; they could wear a happy mask on top of their tragic faces. Each of us, unless he be utterly without feeling, has stored within the deep recesses of his heart feelings of loneliness, a loneliness that cannot be expunged. Each of us is partially or fully incomprehensible to others and is spiritually

cut off from others. Each of us can feel this. The more
the bitter flavor of life is tasted and the more sensitive
a man's feelings become, the more this loneliness will
penetrate down deep into his very bones.

Mu also writes in his preface that all of the scenes and people whom
he describes in these stories are drawn from his own personal
experiences. His own sense of loneliness and alienation may be
attributed to his extremely 'sensitive' perceptions. Indeed, given his
tendency to artfully and creatively blend sensory perceptions into
his fiction, one surmises that Mu himself possessed the rare gift of
synaesthesia, which must also have contributed to his feelings of
isolation and disconnectedness from other human beings.

All of these stories feature women whose relations with men
are ambiguous, unstable, unpredictable and uncontrollable. For
centuries, patriarchal traditions, arranged marriages and the cen-
turies-old practice of foot-binding had kept women firmly in the
'inner quarters' of Chinese family households—save for those who
were sold into the sex trade or entertainment world (which were
often one and the same). Prior to the twentieth century, the idea
of casual romantic relations between unmarried men and women
would have been considered fodder for salacious classical Chinese
novels such as *The Golden Plum Vase* (*Jin ping mei*), *The Carnal
Prayer Mat* (*Rou pu tuan*) or *Dream of the Red Chamber* (*Honglou
meng*), but hardly the stuff of daily life. The May Fourth era of
the 1920s opened the door for new types of relationships to form
between young urbanized men and women. The context for this
change in social and sexual relations was the anonymous existence
of modern metropolitan life. In Shanghai, in particular, but also to
a lesser extent in other large Chinese cities, cultures imported from
the West—particularly institutions of higher education (open to
both sexes), Hollywood films and dance hall culture—encouraged

more fluid and mobile relations between the sexes, greatly enhancing the prospects of choosing romantic and sexual partners prior to or even after marriage, while also fostering heated competition among men for attractive young women, and vice versa. Rivalry and jealousy were the flip side to the expanded sphere of choice available to men and women in Shanghai to pursue romantic affairs.

This new world of dating and night-time leisure had been prefigured to a certain extent by the 'world of flowers' (*huaguo*) that had arisen in the city's two foreign settlements during the late nineteenth century. Indeed, an entire literature had emerged in the late nineteenth century that was focused on the private lives of the city's Chinese courtesans, who worked in numerous private apartments in the foreign settlements. Numerous stories, novels and guidebooks to the city's courtesan culture circulated in those times, peaking with the serial novel *Sing-song Girls of Shanghai* (*Haishang hua liezhuan*), which today is considered by some scholars to be the best Chinese novel written during that century.[15] Courtesans, as scholar Catherine Yeh argues in her book *Shanghai Love*, were the first 'public women' in the modern Chinese city.[16] They established new trends in fashion with their Westernized clothing and hairstyles, they rode around in cars and fancy rickshaws, and they went to public dinner parties and amusement halls while the wives and daughters of the upper classes stayed home. Yet, while courtesans themselves anticipated the modern women of the early twentieth century, they were still caught up in a matrix of rituals, regulations and rules, institutions and associations that placed them squarely within the sex industry.[17]

The face of Shanghai's entertainment world would change in the 1920s as the Western institution of the dance hall and its taxi-dancers entered the city.[18] Fuelled by the new American music known as jazz, Shanghai enjoyed a wave of dance madness that began soon after the end of the First World War in 1919. Not long after that, the call went out for American jazz bands to perform in the city's nightclubs and ballrooms. While some thought that this wave of 'dance madness' would peter out quickly, it endured for the next two decades. While the ballroom dance halls of the city were at first largely the stomping grounds of Westerners living in Shanghai, it did not take long for Western-educated or bohemian Chinese elites to take an interest in the dance craze that was then sweeping the world. By the late 1920s, new dance halls were opening in the city with names like 'Peach Blossom Palace', 'Moon Palace', and 'Black Cat'. This was the first wave of dance halls run and staffed by Chinese rather than Westerners. Most of these dance halls were located in hotels; all of them, without exception, hired young women to serve as dance partners for a largely male clientele. The earliest wave of professional dance partners in the city had been the so-called White Russian women fleeing the Bolshevik Revolution of 1917, who settled in the city by the thousands during the 1920s, but these first Chinese dance halls hired Chinese hostesses instead. Many of these young women, who generally ranged in age from the late teens to the early twenties, were drawn from the 'world of flowers', which was now fading in the city under the onslaught of more modern, commercialized and direct forms of prostitution.[19] Thousands of others were recruited from the surrounding hinterlands to join the growing army of Chinese hostesses that now fox-trotted its way on a nightly basis across the city's polished dance floors.

In terms of her social and sexual roles, the new dance hostess was far more ambiguous than the much older courtesan. These women accompanied men on the dance floor, often helping to teach them how to dance the fox-trot, Charleston, tango or waltz.

They also kept men company at small, intimate tables or on sofas at the edge of the dance hall. Many of these young women were also available, at a price, for a secret rendezvous in a private hotel room or a man's apartment, which greatly enhanced the modest incomes that they earned through collecting dance tickets (as in the taxi-dance halls of the Western world at the time, men paid women one ticket per dance from a book of tickets, which they purchased at the door for a fee). Still, not all women who chose this profession were outright prostitutes; some preferred for patrons to ply them with sentimental gifts (scarves, perfume and the like) and provide them with clothing and private apartments. This system of gift-giving and patronage had been inherited from the 'world of flowers'; it implied a long-term romantic attachment between two consensual partners rather than a brief sexual encounter in exchange for money. Indeed, as Mu Shiying's own story reflects, many of the city's dancers ultimately married one of their male patrons, and thus the world of 1930s social dance halls may be looked upon as a vast dating and marriage market rather than merely a marketplace for quick sexual thrills.

Yet, as elsewhere around the world, the dance hall was also a romantic setting for young Chinese men and women who were stepping into modernity. The figure of the young woman dancing and cavorting freely in the city with men became one of the configurations of the so-called 'modern girl' (*modeng nülang*) in China, explored by Mu and his fellow writers Shi Zhecun, Liu Na'ou and others.[20] In Tokyo, her counterpart was the *modan garu*, who served in cafés as a waitress or else frequented dance halls.[21] The novel *Chijin no ai*, by the famous Japanese writer Tanizaki Junichiro, first published in the mid-1920s as a serial novel, features one such girl named Naomi.[22] The main character of the novel is a man in his thirties who convinces the teenage girl Naomi to live with him as his ward after meeting her in a café where she is working as a waitress. He nurtures her and educates her, and eventually makes her his wife, only to discover years later that she has taken on many young male lovers and has been deceiving him continually whilst cavorting with them behind his back. Naomi is the quintessential *modan garu* or *moga*, who loves to dance, flirt and play with men and who deceptively takes on casual lovers, despite the nurturing and economic support of her hapless husband. Other Japanese writers of the same era such as Nagai Kafu also wrote about Ginza café waitresses and their relations with their male customers, which in some sense echoed earlier types of entertainers such as courtesans and geisha, but in other respects were shockingly modern. The women in Mu Shiying's stories bear some similarities to this Japanese prototype of the *moga*, which may reflect the influence of these writers on Mu and his cohorts as they absorbed modern Japanese literature. Yet, mainly, these similarities are a reflection of the Westernized entertainment industries and cultures that arose simultaneously in both cities during the 1920s and emerged as new arenas for pleasurable activities and sexual conquests for urbanites in Shanghai and Tokyo.

While most of the Chinese dance halls in Shanghai featured professional dance hostesses, the more elite ones did not. Instead, they offered a fantastical setting for Chinese elites to undertake their romantic pursuits. In the 1920s, the leading establishment in this respect was the Majestic Hotel ballroom, which opened its doors in 1925. This ballroom featured a smooth marble dance floor surrounded by pillars, statues and other trappings of Greco-Roman culture. It was designed by a Spanish architect named Lafuente in the shape of a four-leaf clover, boasted a fountain in its centre and was surrounded by lavish dining halls. The establishment also featured an outdoor garden ballroom for the summer months.

This was arguably the first place where Chinese elites learned the arts of Western-style ballroom dancing. The bandleader who performed there nightly, an American by the name of Whitey Smith, later claimed in his memoir that he had 'taught China to dance' by simplifying the complex harmonizations of American jazz and bringing out the melody, while also experimenting with infusions of Chinese folk music into his repertoire.[23] Indeed, an image captured by Fox Movietone Newsreel circa 1929 shows Smith and his band performing in the garden while a group of smartly dressed Chinese couples, the men with slicked-back hair and Western suits, the ladies with *qipaos* and perms, dance gracefully, practising their new steps.[24] These were some of the archetypal images of Chinese modernity that circulated in the West during the 1930s. While the Western-operated Majestic Hotel folded with the onset of the Depression, by the early 1930s, Chinese bankers and businessmen were building their own dance palaces, notably the famous Paramount Ballroom, which opened in 1933, and the Canidrome Ballroom, where the famous Soong sisters learned to tap-dance to the hot tunes of Buck Clayton's Harlem Gentlemen in 1934.[25] In these establishments, elite men and women chose their own dance partners as they mastered the art of ballroom dancing. The women who stepped into these ballrooms were thus participating in a freer, more open and consensual world of courtship, romance and love which had not existed in China one generation before.

This was the 'world of dance' (*wuguo*) into which the dashing young Mu Shiying threw himself in the early 1930s. Following his initial foray with 'Poles Apart' into the ideologically charged world of 'proletarian literature', Mu's subsequent stories, published in literary journals and popular magazines in the early 1930s, focused on the risks of pursuing romantic and sexual liaisons with young men and women who were steeped in the modern and heavily Westernized culture of the metropolis. In these stories, dance halls and hostesses played a central role as the Ur-space of urban modernity. Judging from the experiences and internal worlds of his male characters, Mu clearly viewed sexual attraction and physical consummation of romantic love in the modern urban setting with a contradictory combination of pleasure and trepidation. As exemplified by the stories translated in this book, his characters were constantly on the move, trying to 'hook up' (in our own contemporary parlance) with each other. They did so by creating for themselves a fantastical and phantasmagorical aura of personality in the space of the dance hall, which masked their deep personal flaws and failures, just as the colourful spotlights and dark environments of the city's ballrooms masked the physical flaws and missteps of the dancers. In this sense, Mu's dedication to writing about the torrid affairs of young men and women as they made their way about town reflected his own ironic distancing from the great ideologies of the era. From his writings, it is clear that he saw those who chose to champion these ideologies as hypocrites who masked their own failures, flaws and inadequacies through their heroic and even quixotic stances. This was a subject that Mu even explored in one of his novels, *This Generation of Ours* (*Women zheyidai*, 1936).[26]

Mu's first lengthy exposition of the theme of young romance and the dashing of youthful illusions about love resulted in his rather lengthy short story, 'The Man Who Was Treated as a Plaything'.[27] It is quite possible to imagine that the story is based on Mu's own personal experience with a first-time love affair, which took place while he was a student at Aurora University. This does not mean that the author was simply documenting a personal experience—indeed, he already shows a highly creative sense of time and place, a brilliant knack for dialogue and an inventive storytelling style.

The narrator and primary character, Alexy, is a male university student who falls in love with a female student named Rongzi, only to discover through several painful revelations that she has many other men in her life. One clue that Alexy is none other than the author himself is that, at one point in the story, the girl claims to appreciate his modern writing style—she also mentions enjoying Liu Na'ou and Shi Zhecun, as well as a litany of other modern writers influencing Mu at the time, including the American 'Lost Generation' novelist John Dos Passos. The main tension within the story lies in the narrator's inability to come to terms with the 'lying mouth' of Rongzi, whom he suspects to be carrying on simultaneous affairs with other men as the two build their own romantic relationship. Alexy's naive attempts to control and dominate Rongzi's love life result only in his own frustration and feelings of inadequacy.

Much of the story consists of an ongoing internal monologue, as Alexy debates and discusses Rongzi's intentions and actions with himself. His pursuit of the girl involves strategies of courtship and romance that were probably circulating at the time through the influence of the Hollywood film culture pervading the city in that era. Indeed, he frequently likens Rongzi to various Hollywood female icons from the age, from Vilma Banky to Clara Bow. Clearly, he is casting her in a role as femme fatale that is largely based on female characters from the world of cinema. It is a role that she is ill fit for, as he discovers over time. Alexy courts Rongzi by taking long evening strolls, relaxing in the countryside, taking a rowboat ride in a pond and quoting foreign poetry. Yet their dialogue is full of innuendoes alluding to her misbehaviour with other male suitors. They adopt the metaphor of consumption to discuss her relations with other men, which the narrator likens to eating too many different types of snacks, which gives her indigestion. The humour of the story is childish and even scatalogical—she claims that she is 'constipated' and has trouble passing these 'snacks' through her alimentary canal. For her, the young poet and writer is a welcome 'stimulant' to restore her jaded appetite. Alexy suggests that she watch her diet more carefully, implying that she discard the other men who are taking up space in her busy social life, and 'go steady' with him instead. One can easily imagine that such a plot came up frequently in the Hollywood films of that time, as they still do now.

As the story unfolds along with their relationship, constructed out of idle fantasies of love and fidelity on the part of the narrator (the English term *fidelity* is even used in the story), the setting shifts back and forth between the bucolic countryside and the hustle and bustle of the big city. Fields, parks, rivers and trees dominate the scenery of the former, while the latter is filled with dance halls, cars and crowded avenues. While one might construe the countryside as representing purity and innocence—and indeed, such is the mentality of the young, naive narrator—while the city connotes decadence, sin and excess, the dichotomy is not so simply conceived. For it is in a country setting that Alexy, whilst rowing a boat on a pond, discovers his girl on a romantic boat ride with a male rival. Characteristically, she hops out of the rival's boat and into Alexy's, despite his great shame and embarrassment, such that he tries to hide himself on the floor of the boat. Once she is ensconced in his boat, the other man sulkily rows away.

The easy transfer of the girl from one man's boat to another's becomes a metaphor for the emotional journey of lovers from partner to partner in the modern city. This is echoed in the way that dancers in a dance hall switch partners—a subject that fascinated and entranced Mu to no end. Mu himself was noted to be a great dancer, certainly the most avid one among the crowd of avant-garde writers with which he ran. One reflection of his life reminisced, 'Whenever the sky began to grow dark, Mu would make his way to the "Moon Palace Dance Hall" wearing a Western suit, with a tall frame, the dashing figure that Mu Shiying cut on the dance floor caused people to regard him with awe, for he and his dancing partner were always the best dancers on the floor.'[28] In one of the climactic scenes of 'Plaything', Alexy makes the rounds of dance halls, drinking heavily while searching for his lover who has disappeared, only to find her dancing with another man. He becomes violent and enraged, showing the vivid colours of his jealousy in a public display that he later regrets. The relationship becomes a tug of war, with Alexy trying to assert his masculine hegemony over the woman he has 'hunted' and 'captured', only to question whether it is she who is the hunter and he the 'prey'. Indeed, the story continually questions and interrogates the gendered expectations and behaviours of man and woman, not to mention broad concepts such as love and faith.

In this story, we learn very little of the interior life of the girl Rongzi, who reveals her own situation and motivations near the end of the tale, only to conceal them once again by claiming to be joking. Like the narrator, we are left without knowing what is truth and what is merely fiction. (We leave it to the reader to discover for him-or herself how the story ends.) At many times during the tale, we find Alexy hanging out by her dorm window, suggesting a voyeuristic desire to peer inside her interior world, but he never really discovers her true nature or her own complex motivations for seeking the company of men. In one of the final scenes, he is still hanging outside her window, but her room is empty.

These themes of unrequited or unfulfilled love, desire, longing and loss are repeated frequently throughout Mu's early works. While one does not wish to read everything in his stories as metaphorical or allegorical, we can certainly map his works onto the city and its antithesis, the countryside, on multiple levels. For these are the two fundamental dichotomies that Mu works with in his stories. The possession of the woman, the ferreting out of her deepest secrets, can be likened to the colonization of the fertile countryside by the male force of industrialization and urbanization. The city of Shanghai can thus be read as a masculine entity, rather than the feminine entity that many others have envisioned. Shanghai, the colonizer, is ever stretching its tentacles outward, gripping the country that surrounds it with the madness of capitalist urban modernity, just as the colonizers themselves—the British, French, Americans and others who constitute the implicit backdrop to his stories of city life—are constantly stretching their power outward to embrace and map the surrounding hinterlands. One image in his story 'Shanghai Fox-trot' stands out here: that of the famous character on the Johnnie Walker signboard 'still going strong' as he tries to gain a foothold in the surrounding territories. Certainly, Mu was well aware of the anti-colonialist discourse that had evolved since the May Fourth era and which was hammering louder and louder on the doors of the semi-colonial metropolis in the new age of Chinese nationalism. Ironically, Mu would later join forces with the man who ultimately did secure the return of Shanghai to Chinese sovereignty in 1943: Wang Jingwei. Yet he would pay for that decision with his life, and would not live to witness that historic event.

Returning to the theme of colonization through the metaphorical conquest of the female body, we are reminded of one key passage from his story 'Craven "A"'.[29] In this tale, the narrator pursues a dance hall hostess whom he nicknames 'Craven "A"' after her favourite cigarette brand. It is no coincidence that he chose this brand, since Mu himself was reputed to be a big fan of it.[30] He must also have been aware of the connotations of the word 'craven', since Mu was also well versed in English. Indeed, his stories are shot through with English phrases, which we have indicated in bold letters in the text of the translations. Early in the story, while gazing at the dance hostess he calls 'Craven "A"', the narrator imagines her body as a foreign country to be conquered by the colonialist male adventurer. From head to toe, he maps out the terrain of her body in great and telling detail, likening her breasts to twin mountains, while the erogenous zone between her legs is imagined as a port city, with the phallic imagery of 'majestic ships' sailing in to dock at its harbour. Whether based on Shanghai or Hong Kong (a city that he also spent time in later on in his brief life), this vision of the port city as a vaginal entry zone into the imaginary country stands out as one of the great metaphors of his storytelling career.

As the story proceeds, the narrator, a well-off lawyer who lives in a Western-style apartment building, conquers and 'captures' the girl, taking her to his flat for easy, casual sex. He then enjoys a smoke while looking out over the urban landscape. In the narrator's imagination, the girl becomes limp and lifeless, like a store-front mannequin or an automaton. Meanwhile, the city itself becomes a living body, whose veins and arteries are the head-and taillights of the rushing traffic. Like the city of Shanghai, a foreign territory to be conquered by the modern Chinese adventurer, the body of 'Craven "A"' is a terrain that many of his friends have already explored, choosing to remain there for a brief spell before moving on to other conquests. Unlike the naive young Alexy of 'Plaything', the narrator of 'Craven "A"' is more seasoned and more jaded—clearly reflecting Mu's own advancement into the realm of

Shanghai nightlife. By the end of the story, he receives some revelations about the relations that 'Craven "A"' has had with other men and does succeed in peeking more deeply into her interior world, as she invites him into her home and shows him photographs of other men who had courted her in the past.

Unlike Rongzi, the college girl, 'Craven "A"' is a dance hostess, and thus is not expected to be pure and pristine. In fact, her chosen job is to seduce and be seduced by men in the dance hall. Whether that seduction carries on into private bedrooms is another story, since, as pointed out earlier, dance hostesses occupied an ambiguous terrain within the city's vast sexual service industry. Mu himself was so fascinated by the allure of dance hostesses that he eventually married a Cantonese dancer named Qiu Peipei, whom he met at the Moon Palace Dance Hall in the Hongkou district of the city. The struggles that his male narrators undergo in their stories may reflect his own internal conflicts as he courted a woman of the night who danced and drank with many other men, and struggled to make her his own. This struggle would last throughout their marriage, since apparently she did not give up her career as a dancer even after moving to Hong Kong in 1936. Yet the struggle also went the other way, as Mu continued to frequent dance halls and dance with many other hostesses.

Generally speaking, the voices in these stories by Mu Shiying are those of the young well-to-do men of a certain generation who found themselves uneasy with the idea of women charting their own independent sexual trajectories as they made their way through the novel terrain of the modern metropolis. The masculine urge to pin down, classify, control and regulate female sexuality, present in all modern cities, is clearly reflected in this set of tales.[31] One might go so far as to provide a biological explanation for this desire—women always know that the child born to them is their own, whereas men can never be one hundred percent sure of their fatherhood (at least, not until the advent of paternity tests)—but to do so oversimplifies the complex social, political, economic and cultural frameworks that support the ever-shifting notions of masculinity and femininity in the modern metropolis. Still, it is very clear from these stories that Mu was wrestling with his own masculine identity as he came of age in the metropolis. Alexy strikes the reader as a weak and effeminate—and certainly oversensitive—young man, the typical romantic image of a poet, while the narrator of 'Craven "A"' and the sailor in the story 'Night' express their male virility through their studied conquests of women. On a spectrum of masculinity, one could claim that Alexy has the most feminine attributes, the lawyer in 'Craven "A"' lies somewhere in the middle (he is still sensitive but not overly so), while the anonymous sailor of 'Night' shows the highest level of masculinity in his persona—but not so much as to be beyond displaying some of his own sentimentality towards the woman he conquers in this story, who also happens to be a jaded dance hall girl.

By the time Mu was writing the stories collected in this book, dance hostesses had become a fixture of the city's urban culture. Not only did they appear by the thousands nightly in the city's cabarets, but they also popped up frequently in the visual and textual realms of film, fiction and pop magazines that were circulating throughout the city during that period.[32] With her ambiguous position in the urban schema—not quite actress, not quite prostitute, not quite society girl—the dance hostess created enormous thrills and great anxieties for men who wished to pin down her identity. Even the governments that ruled over the city struggled in the effort to control and regulate the social and sexual personae of dance hostesses within an official ideological language, creating a system of licensing and regulations that by the 1940s became so cumbersome that it nearly brought the entire dance hall industry down.[33] Mu's meditations on the inner struggles of men like Alexy, the narrator of 'Craven "A"', the sailor in 'Night' and the men in the story 'Black Peony' thus represent a broader social movement at a crucial period of transformation in the urban culture of modern China.

The personal struggles that Mu's male and female characters undergo in his stories are thus indicative of a broader sea change in Chinese urban culture during the Republican era, in which young educated urban elites sought out their own romantic and marital partners outside of the more traditional dichotomies of wife/ family and courtesan/concubine. Until the 1920s—and, for most of China, well beyond that period—the norm was for parents to arrange marriages for their children. Marriage was not a romantic partnership but rather an economic exchange and a corporate alliance between families. Wives were expected to play roles in bearing children, particularly male heirs, and contributing to the household economy. Sex was largely constructed as a procreative act, rather than an emotional union between a couple. Certainly, there were other discourses: by the Ming dynasty, pornographic literature was a distinctive feature of the country's vast literary landscape, but by the Qing, these sexual excesses were reined in and Confucian norms enforced throughout the realm.[34] This helps to explain why Shanghai, with its foreign enclaves, became a leading centre for prostitution during a period in which courtesan culture was more greatly suppressed elsewhere in China.[35] Naturally, in Chinese civilization, there were many variations on the theme of human sexuality and on sexual relations and gender roles over the centuries, but the persistence of the traditions that fit into the ideological framework of Confucianism, and other practices such as foot-binding that were designed to keep women immobile, were remarkable and distinctive features of Chinese culture.[36]

The watershed May Fourth period and the associated New Culture movement challenged these traditions, as a new generation of Western-educated professors and impressionable, fiery youths fought for their own personal emancipation from the 'shackles' of the 'feudal' Confucian system. This was true for the most part in large urban enclaves such as Shanghai, less so in the vast hinterlands which maintained the patriarchal traditions up through the Communist Revolution of 1949. Meanwhile, changes in the legal system such as the new marriage laws under the Nationalist government, which came to power in 1927, encouraged Chinese to embark on a course towards monogamous marital unions and shed the ages-old system of polygamy, which had enabled wealthy men to accrue several female partners (a principal wife and multiple concubines) for the purposes of showcasing their status, enhancing their personal pleasures, and ensuring the birth of male heirs to the family estate. Over the next three years, between 1928 and 1931, new laws were promulgated by the national government to reform family law and provide women with more support within the institution of the family. Concubines were not eradicated but their lots were arguably improved by the new laws, and women were given the right to divorce in the case of undesirable marriages. Although it is not clear whether these laws had a wide-ranging transformative effect, they certainly set a new tone for male-female relations.[37] As the country lurched towards modernity, new romantic ideas concerning the foundations of a marital union came to the fore in Chinese intellectual and political discourse, grounded in Western notions of romantic love and free choice of marital partner rather than the economic imperatives of household enrichment and the perpetuation of one's patrilineage.[38]

Mu and his fellow writers found themselves caught up in this social, political and cultural sea change. Mu himself was too young to participate in the May Fourth movement, which broke out in 1919 when he was merely seven, but he certainly was well aware of May Fourth discourse, which was as active in the universities and streets of Shanghai as it was in Beijing and elsewhere. His educational background was shared by a generation of elite university students who had been "alienated" from both their own cultural traditions as well as the political ideologies of the age, particularly after the violent revolution of 1927 disenfranchised many intellectuals and university students from the national revolutionary movement.[39] Living in a semi-colonial environment and attending a French Jesuit college, Mu and his classmates were thrust into a world of ambiguities and contradictions as they wrestled with their own social and cultural identities as modern Chinese urbanites. His writings are a rich and dense portrayal of the inner and outer worlds of young men and women seeking to master the new environment of a modern, internationalized metropolis while also questioning their own cultural heritage and their inherited value systems.

Yet despite the veneer of romance and adventure that coated the new relations between the sexes, Mu was painfully aware that economic forces still undergirded these relations. The physical and intellectual attraction of a young poet or writer might suffice to lure a girl into a rendezvous or a brief courtship, but diamonds and furs, a villa in the countryside and other things that a wealthy man supplied were far more likely to win a woman's heart than the ability to quote a few English poems or speak in *bon mots*. In 'Plaything', Alexy soon learns of his own relative value as Rongzi tells him of her other older, wealthier and more powerful suitors. As the son of a failed banker who had died of depression, Mu was well aware of his own precarious financial situation. It is no coincidence that one of the characters in his story 'Five in a Nightclub' is also a gold speculator who goes bankrupt and shoots himself in a spectacular suicide scene at the end of the story. His partner at the nightclub, Daisy Huang, is also a has-been, a not-so-young socialite who is painfully aware of her fading value in the sexual marketplace. The two are intentionally paired, showing the ephemerality of wealth and beauty. After all, a fortune painfully acquired by a man through many years of hard work can be lost in a few days of reckless gambling. Meanwhile, women who were the talk of the town one year, whether as actresses, dancers, socialites or courtesans, are quickly replaced by younger ones in a city in which the age of twenty-five was generally considered the endpoint of a woman's career in public sociability. Mu here reflects critically on the endless circulation and exchange of capital, coin, fashion and images of beauty that characterize the life of the modern city.

This helps to explain the odd trajectory of the story 'Black Peony'. This story, published in 1934 in the popular magazine *Liangyou*, or 'Good Companion', is one of his more approachable tales, characteristically filled with linguistic goodies that must have pleased its many readers. Black Peony, who appears in illustrations in the magazine, is the name given to a certain dance hostess whom the male narrator befriends at the beginning of the tale. Like many of his other femme fatales, she has an appearance that mixes and mingles aspects of both East and West. The two characters share the same sense of ennui and fatigue that comes from living in the modern city, with its endless supply of luxuries and novelties: 'Take me for example, I'm living in the lap of luxury, if you take away jazz, fox-trot, mixed drinks, the fashionable colours of autumn, eight-cylinder engine cars, Egyptian tobacco . . . I become a soulless person. So deeply soaked in luxury, *carpe diem*, I am living this life of luxury, but I am tired.'

Later, while contemplating another weekend of nightclubbing, the narrator receives an invitation from an old friend named Shengwu, to see a 'black peony' that has miraculously 'blossomed' in the garden of his countryside villa. This turns out to be none other than the dancer he had met and with whom he had shared a momentary sense of camaraderie during a previous evening. She confides in him and shares the secret of her mysterious journey to the countryside into the arms of her rescuer, Shengwu. Apparently she has found her Shangri-la in the bucolic surroundings of a country villa as the new wife of its well-to-do owner, while the narrator himself must return to the hustle and bustle of the great metropolis, even if it kills him. He uses the metaphor of ants to describe the sensation of being crushed by the trivialities of life, comparing them to the number 3. 'There are 333333333333 crawling onto me from all directions without stopping, and I can't get away from them. I'm crushed! I'm really crushed by them! I walk back into life, and as for that white room, the flower garden, the violets hanging in pearl-like chains in front of the patio, the fruity scent of the grape arbour . . . I must throw it all behind me. But one day I'll collapse in the middle of the road!' So ends the story: in this plaintive cry, we hear the voice of Mu himself as he struggled to interpret the banality of his own existence as a modern Chinese urbanite, caught up in a cauldron of revolutionary forces that were far beyond his control.

Following the publication of *Public Cemetery* in 1933, Mu published two more collections of short stories: *Platinum Statue of a Female Nude* (*Baijin de nüti suxiang*, 1934) and *Saint Virgin's Love* (*Sheng chunü de ganqing*, 1935), as well as numerous short stories, essays and other odds and ends published in various journals and magazines. Mu's own personal trajectory eventually took him to Hong Kong, before his fateful return to Shanghai to serve the Wang Jingwei 'puppet' regime. While one might imagine that the pressures of the wartime era drove him to seek refuge in the British colony, one Hong Kong journalist tells another story.[40] The writer Ye Lingfeng had given Mu the contact information for a Hong Kong–based journalist named Lü Lun in the hope that he could help Mu to find a job with his newspaper there. Lü Lun claims that Mu travelled to Hong Kong in the summer of 1936 in order to reunite with his estranged wife, Qiu Peipei. It seems that the two had had a falling out in Shanghai, whereupon she decided to move to Hong Kong and live with her sister. The distraught Mu followed his loved one south to the colony, where they were indeed reunited—but only after he lived up to his promise to shave his head as a punishment for some infraction that we shall never know about. Indeed, in Hong Kong, Mu continued to publish essays and stories which became more overtly political as the Japanese empire stretched its ominous shadow over China. Meanwhile, his wife Qiu Peipei continued her work as a dance hostess in Hong Kong's dance hall scene. Her move to the colonial city was part of a mass migration of entertainment industry people from Shanghai to Hong Kong during the war years, which greatly elevated the film, dance and other industries in the 'Fragrant Harbour'. Mu continued to make a living as a writer, but the two fell on hard times as the war pressed on.

It is not entirely clear why Mu chose to return to Shanghai in 1939 as an agent of the newly formed Wang Jingwei collaborationist government. Records left by Japanese writers whom he visited in Tokyo during that year indicate that he went to Japan as part of a delegation of journalists. Apparently he had grown out his hair again to suitable length, since the Japanese writers invariably described him as a dashing and charming fellow who lit up the parties to which he was invited with conversation and wit. Mu apparently felt that, by winning over the hearts and minds of his Japanese counterparts in the world of letters, he could bridge cultural differences and pave the way to a better understanding between the nations, which might in turn mitigate the calamitous war that was ongoing in his home country. He even chose not to protect himself with bodyguards despite the warnings of his colleagues. For this idealism, he paid dearly with his young life.[41]

Following his assassination, the newspaper for which he had worked, the *Guomin ribao*, published an article detailing the circumstances of his death. Interestingly, the article does not mention his unique contributions to modern Chinese literature. Instead, it focuses on his career as an agent of the Wang regime. The article was brought to the attention of the Shanghai Municipal Police, which produced an English translation for their files. Given that this is a rare unpublished document, it is worth reproducing in its entirety for the reader of this book; despite its obvious propagandistic intent and the paucity of its contents regarding his meteoric career in letters, it may serve as an obituary of sorts for the enigmatic figure of Mu Shiying:

(Shanghai Municipal Police file D8149.C.768 dated July 1, 1940)

June 29, 1940. Morning Translation.

Kuo Min Daily News publishes the following report as captioned:

'General Manager of This Paper Murdered'

At 6:40 p.m. yesterday while Moh Shih-ying [Mu Shiying], general manager of this paper, was passing the vicinity of Lane 195, Fokien Road, in a rickshaw on his way to Nanking Road, he was shot at by desperadoes. Moh was taken by surprise. He was wounded in the right shoulder and in the right abdomen, and collapsed. The desperadoes had already made good their escape when the post duty policemen in the vicinity rushed up to the scene.

Upon receipt of a report, a large party of detectives and policemen from Louza Police Station arrived at the scene in riot vans and an ambulance was summoned immediately to remove the wounded man to the Lester Chinese Hospital, but owing to the serious nature of his wounds and to the loss of blood, Moh died upon arrival at the hospital.

The coolie of the rickshaw in which Mr. Moh was riding was wounded in the right leg.

A hawker selling peaches at the entrance of Lane 195, Fokien Road, who saw the desperadoes doing the shooting, said: 'There were two men in the case. One held a pistol and opened fire, while the other gave directions by his side. The man who opened fire was dressed in a blue foreign-style shirt with canvass foreign-style trousers. The desperado who gave directions by his side was attired in a blue long gown. They took to their heels upon seeing that their object had been attained.'

The hawker, who is an eye-witness of the murder, was taken to the Police Station by detectives and policemen for interrogation. The wounded rickshaw coolie was also taken to the Police Station after first being given treatment at the Lester Chinese Hospital. The Police are making discrete [*sic*] investigations in an effort to arrest the murderers.

People in various circles of life became much excited upon learning of the murder of Mr. Moh.

Mr. Moh, a native of Sz Chi, Chekiang, age 29, was a graduate of Kwang Hwa [Guanghua] University. When Chairman Wang Ching-wei [Wang Jingwei] issued the telegram advocating a peace movement, Mr. Moh was in Hongkong and immediately joined the movement. He came to Shanghai in autumn last year at the close of the Sixth Plenary Congress and joined the Ministry of Publicity at Nanking. He undertook the formation of this paper and most of its comments and articles were written by him. In Shanghai he undertook the work of a special deputy of the Ministry of Publicity following the return of the National Government to Nanking. He was careful and diligent in his work, but was hated by reactionary desperadoes.

On June 20, this paper received a threatening letter by post, expressing the hope that this paper would change its attitude in the work of propagating peace. The letter was taken to Louza Police Station on June 22. Since then, every day this Police Station has been detailing two policemen to the office of this paper to accord protection.

Prior to his leaving China together with the Goodwill Mission, Mr. Moh's family received a strange telephone call, warning him to sever his connection with the peace movement front at once, failing which his life would be in danger. On the very day that Mr. Moh returned to China from Japan, his family received a similar telephone call. His family advised him to be careful of his movements, but he paid no heed saying that since he had offered himself to the Kuomintang Government, he would do his best for the peace movement, and that he cared nothing for his life.

The death of Mr. Moh is not only a loss to this paper; it is a loss also to China.

Notes

1. The flourishing of interest in Mu among Chinese scholars also precipitated interest in him and other 'new sensationalist' writers in Western academia. A good biographical account of Mu Shiying in English appears in Shu-mei Shi, *The Lure of the Modern: Writing Modernism in Semicolonial China, 1917–1937* (Berkeley: University of California Press, 2001). Leo Ou-fan Lee analyses Mu's works in his *Shanghai Modern: The Flowering of a New Urban Culture in China, 1930–1945* (Cambridge, MA: Harvard University Press, 1999).

2. Yan Jiayan and Li Jin (eds.), *The Collected Works of Mu Shiying* (*Mu Shiying quanji*), vols. 1–3 (Beijing: Beijing chubanshe, 2008).

3. For a full account of this war, see Donald A. Jordan, *China's Trial by Fire: The Shanghai War of 1932* (Ann Arbor: University of Michigan, 2001).

4. Kang Yi (Ji Kangyi), 'Hearing a Flute at Shanyang: Remembering the 1930s New Sensationalist Writer Mr. Mu Shiying' (Lindi shanyang: daonian yiwei sanshi niandai xin'ganjuepai zuojia Mu Shiying xiansheng), *Anecdotes* (*Zhanggu*) 10 (1972): 48–50, referenced in Shi, *The Lure of the Modern*, 308.

5. The phrase 'literary comet' was used by Ye Lingfeng to describe Mu's career. See 'A Comet in the 1930s Literary Arena: Ye Lingfeng Talks about Mu Shiying' (Sanshi niandai wentan shang de yike huixing: Ye Lingfeng xiansheng tan Mu Shiying), *Four Seasons* (*Siji*) 1 (November 1972): 30.

6. The most recent compilation is a full collection of his entire works as well as articles about Mu Shiying, letters and other documents compiled by the scholar Yan Jiayan. See Yan and Li, *The Collected Works of Mu Shiying*.

7. Wu Huanzhang (ed.), *Selected Stories of the Shanghai School* (*Haipai xiaoshuo jingpin*) (Shanghai: Fudan University Press, 1996).

8. Zhang Ailing (Eileen Chang), 'Little Brother' (Didi), in *Heaven and Earth Monthly (Tiandi yuekan)* nos. 7–8, May 1944, reprinted in *Complete Essays by Eileen Chang (Zhang Ailing sanwen quanbian)* (Hohhot: Neimenggu wenhua chubanshe, 1996), 103–5. In this short

piece about her brother, she mentions that she was reading Mu's story 'Poles Apart' as well as a story by the writer Ba Jin.

9. Wu Huanzhang, preface, *Selected Stories of the Shanghai School*, 11.

10. Shi, *The Lure of the Modern*, 286.

11. In her own brilliant analysis of Mu's life and works, the Chinese scholar Shu-mei Shi likens the shifting of scenes and perspectives in 'Shanghai Fox-trot' to camera movements on a film set. See Shi, *The Lure of the Modern*, 326–8.

12. For studies of the city's gangland underworld and its relations with the city police and the Nationalist government, see Brian Martin, *The Shanghai Green Gang: Politics and Organized Crime, 1919–1937* (Berkeley: University of California Press, 1997) and Frederic Wakeman, *Policing Shanghai, 1927–1937* (Berkeley: University of California Press, 1995).

13. The classic study in English-language scholarship of this movement is Chow Tse-tsung, *The May Fourth Movement: Intellectual Revolution in Modern China* (Cambridge, MA: Harvard University Press, 1960). See also Vera Schwarcz, *The Chinese Enlightenment: Intellectuals and the Legacy of the May Fourth Movement of 1919* (Berkeley: University of California Press, 1986).

14. Mu Shiying, 'Preface to Public Cemetery', translated by Kirk A. Denton, in *Modern Chinese Literary Thought: Writings on Literature, 1893–1945*, edited by Kirk A. Denton (Stanford, CA: Stanford University Press, 1996), 387–9; 389.

15. For a translation of this famous novel, see Han Bangqing, *The Sing-song Girls of Shanghai* (New York: Columbia University Press, 2012); David Der-wei Wang, *Fin-de-Siècle Splendor: Repressed Modernities of Late Qing Fiction, 1849–1911* (Palo Alto, CA: Stanford University Press, 1997), features a discussion of this novel and other late Qing courtesan novels.

16. Catherine Vance Yeh, *Shanghai Love: Courtesans, Intellectuals, and Entertainment Culture, 1850–1910* (Seattle: University of Washington Press, 2006).

17. For other accounts of courtesan culture in Shanghai and changes to that culture in the wake of the city's modernization in the early

twentieth century, see Christian Henriot, *Prostitution and Sexuality in Shanghai: A Social History, 1849–1949* (Cambridge: Cambridge University Press, 2001) and Gail Hershatter, *Dangerous Pleasures: Prostitution and Modernity in Twentieth-Century Shanghai* (Berkeley: University of California Press, 1996).

18. The history of Shanghai cabarets is discussed at length in Andrew David Field, *Shanghai's Dancing World: Cabaret Culture and Urban Politics, 1919–1954* (Hong Kong: Chinese University Press, 2010).

19. This process is neatly summarized in Christian Henriot, 'From a Throne of Glory to a Seat of Ignominy: Prostitution Revisited (1849– 1949)', *Modern China* 22 (1996): 132–63.

20. The 'modern girl' and 'new woman' were figures that emerged in China in the early twentieth century. The former had a strong sexual connotation and was modelled loosely on the American 'flapper girl', while the latter had more of a political connotation suggesting a woman who was entering public affairs and eschewing traditional female roles. See Sarah E. Stevens, 'Figuring Modernity: The New Woman and the Modern Girl in Republican China', *NWSA Journal* 15, no. 3 (Autumn, 2003): 82–103.

21. For accounts of 1920s Tokyo café culture and the waitresses who worked in the cafés of Ginza and elsewhere, see Miriam Silverberg, 'The Café Waitress Serving Modern Japan', in *Mirror of Modernity: Invented Traditions of Modern Japan*, edited by Stephen Vlastos (Berkeley: University of California Press, 1998), 208–25. See also Miriam Silverberg, 'The Modern Girl as Militant', in *Recreating Japanese Women, 1600–1945*, edited by Gail Bernstein (Berkeley: University of California Press, 1991), 239–40; and Elise Tipton, 'Pink Collar Work: The Café Waitress in Early Twentieth Century Japan', in *Intersections: Gender, History and Culture in the Asian Context*, Issue 7, March 2002 (http://intersections.anu.edu.au/issue7/tipton. html). For a broader account of the 'new woman' in interwar Japan, see Barbara Sato, *The New Japanese Woman: Modernity, Media and Women in Interwar Japan* (London: Duke University Press, 2003).

22. For an English translation of this novel, see Tanizaki Junichiro, *Naomi* (New York: Vintage, 2001).

23. Whitey Smith with C. L. McDermott, *I Didn't Make a Million* (Manila: Philippine Education Company, 1956).

24. I have put this film clip up as a Youtube video along with Whitey Smith's song 'Nighttime in Old Shanghai', at http://www.youtube.com/watch?v=6g8yjzPD5cs&lr=1.

25. Buck Clayton with Nancy Miller Elliot, *Buck Clayton's Jazz World* (New York: Oxford University Press, 1987), Chapter 4, 'Shanghai'.

26. This novel is discussed in Shi, *The Lure of the Modern*, 315.

27. The title itself is ambiguous. It has also been translated as 'Men Kept as Playthings' (Shi, *The Lure of the Modern*, 310). Since the Chinese language does not normally denote plurality or verb tense except in context, the title could be read either way. Our own choice puts the focus of the title firmly on the male protagonist, Alexy, who is a thinly veiled stand-in for the author himself.

28. Zheng Zeqing, 'Mu Shiying: The Destiny of an Author of a Western Adventurers' Metropolis' (Mu Shiying: Yige yangchang zuojia de guisu), in *New Literature Historical Documents* (*Xin wenxue shiliao*) 1986, no. 1, quoted in Li Honghua, *Shanghai Culture and Modernistic Literature* (*Shanghai wenhua yu xiandaipai wenxue*) (Nanchang: Jiangxi renmin chubanshe, 2010).

29. Both Leo Ou-fan Lee and Shu-mei Shi analyse this passage in their books on Shanghai literary modernism. See Lee, *Shanghai Modern*, 215–17, and Shi, *The Lure of the Modern*, 318–20. Shi also provides her own translation of this passage in her book.

30. Hei Ying, 'The Mu Shiying I Knew' (Wo jiandao de Mu Shiying), *Historical Materials on Modern Chinese Literature* (February 1989): 142–5, referenced in Shih, *The Lure of the Modern*, 305.

31. See Elizabeth Wilson, *The Sphinx in the City: Urban Life, Control of Disorder, and Women* (Berkeley: University of California Press, 1992).

32. Again, I refer the reader to my book *Shanghai's Dancing World* for further information on the plethora of Chinese press coverage that this world received in Shanghai during the 1930s and 1940s.

33. See *Shanghai's Dancing World*, particularly the later chapters for a

full account of how the city's dance industry was over-regulated and nearly destroyed during the 1940s.

34. Matthew Sommer, *Sex, Law and Society in Late Imperial China* (Stanford, CA: Stanford University Press, 2000).

35. Again, I refer the reader to the aforementioned studies by Henriot, Hershatter and Yeh respectively on the city's courtesan culture in the late Qing and early Republican periods.

36. For an excellent overview of changes in female gender roles in China over the longue durée, see Patricia Ebrey, 'Women, Marriage, and the Family in Chinese History', in *Heritage of China: Contemporary Perspectives on Chinese Civilization*, edited by Paul Ropp (Berkeley: University of California Press, 1990), 197–223.

37. For a discussion of these new laws and their effect on Chinese society, see Peter Zarrow, *China in War and Revolution, 1895–1949* (New York: Routledge, 2005), 261–2. For a study of divorce in that era, see Kathryn Bernhardt, 'Women and the Law: Divorce in the Republican Period', in *Civil Law in Qing and Republican China*, edited by Kathryn Bernhardt and Philip C. C. Huang (Stanford, CA: Stanford University Press, 1994), 187–214.

38. See Wen-hsin Yeh, *The Alienated Academy: Culture and Politics in Republican China, 1919–1937* (Cambridge, MA: Harvard University Press, 1990), 255–6; see also Schwarcz, *The Chinese Enlightenment*, 115–7.

39. Wen-hsin Yeh, *The Alienated Academy*, particularly Chapter 7.

40. Lü Lun, 'Mu Shiying in Hong Kong' (Mu Shiying zai Xianggang), in Lü Lun, *Writings from the Watery Room* (*Xiang shuiwu biyu*) (Hong Kong: Sanlian shudian, 1985), reprinted in Yan and Li, *The Collected Works of Mu Shiying*, vol. 3, 527–9.

41. See Shi, *The Lure of the Modern*, 331–8, for a discussion of the articles published by Japanese writers after Mu's assassination in 1940, detailing their recollections of his visits to Japan. Translations of these articles into Chinese can be found in Yan and Li, *The Collected Works of Mu Shiying*, vol. 3.

1

The Man Who Was Treated as a Plaything
被當作消遣品的男子 (1933)

Written while Mu was attending the prestigious Aurora College, this story appears to be a semi-autobiographical account of the author's first foray into the treacherous world of modern romantic love. The story follows the troublesome courtship of a female college classmate named Rongzi by a young Chinese man who goes by the name of Alexy. The story itself maps out a terrain of romantic engagements and entanglements across the playing field of the city. The narrator grudgingly and unwillingly competes with many other men who also vie for the young woman's affections.

Told from the male narrator's point of view, the woman appears to be both mysterious and untrustworthy. At one point, he even pursues her into the tumultuous world of night-time cabarets, where he entangles himself in a forest of dancing legs while searching for his girl, only to find her inevitably in another man's arms. One of the main tensions within the story lies in the narrator's unsuccessful attempt to convince the girl to remain faithful to him.

In this story, the dimensions of fidelity are ambiguous. It is never entirely clear how physically intimate the two become during their time together. The question of female chastity underscores this relationship. Chastity for women was an age-old value in Confucian China. Yet the onslaught of a Westernized modernity of consumption and leisure in the semi-colonial city, exemplified by Hollywood films and products such as lipstick (the brand here is Tangee) challenged the old norms.

In Shanghai, women were often treated as sexualized commodities; prostitution was rife. Caught in such an urban milieu, it was difficult for women not to commodify themselves sexually in order to receive the gifts of affection and attention from men. On the other hand, young women who attended elite schools of higher learning were part of a larger movement to liberate women from the shackles of Confucian-style oppression. Their sexual liberation was part and parcel of this process.

Rongzi appears in this story as a sexually liberated woman, not simply a girl trying to make a living through her body. One feels the tensions inherent in this sea change in roles for women, as a young man comes to terms with the freedom of choice that a young woman possesses. Whether Rongzi represents only a small set of elite, Westernized girls in the modern metropolis, or whether her experience was one that was shared by the broader masses of young women finding their way through the matrix of modern urban life is a question for social historians of modern China to ponder for decades to come.

The Man Who Was Treated as a Plaything

That day when I returned to my dormitory, I thought of your talkative lips, and was so dazed in amazement that for half a day I forgot my hunger. I gazed at the blue sky, thinking about what a great talker you would be if you were with your lover. And this monastic life I lead, how lonely it is.

If I keep going this way, my soul will become fossilized . . . but please come see me one more time! Rongzi.

Like Clara Bow, the words waltz happily across the peach-coloured paper. They surround me—'Yikes!' I begin to fear.

The first time I met her, I felt, 'What a dangerous animal!' She had a snake's body, a cat's head, a mixture of the gentle and the dangerous. Wearing a long red silk *qipao*, like she was standing on a light breeze, the corners of her *qipao* floating. One look at her feet and I could tell that she was a dancer, stepping around in red silk high heels that were as lovely as crabapple flowers. One imagined her waist as the neck of a vase, from the top bloomed a glimmering peony flower . . . a mouth that told lies, a pair of trickster's eyes—a precious object!

I, who had been fooled in the past, fully understood that such an upfront person as myself could not deal with girls whose mouths told lies. I had met her only three times, and always kept on the alert, hearing her blather along, while from her mouth issued forth the Suzhou accent. Could this innocent mouth also speak lies? Perhaps it could—with my will-power, I built a high wall between myself and her. The first time she attacked me without holding back. Up till now, this dangerous animal consorted with me as if we'd been old friends for ten years. 'This time I won't be fooled again, eh? It wasn't me who chased her, it was she who had seized me!' Every time I returned home and lay down on my bed I would thus dissect the matter.

To go see her again would be very dangerous! When it came down to love, I was simply a moron. Without much thought, I had written her back: 'Work has been extremely busy.' Actually I was about to take a bath. Returning from the study, combing my hair, I suddenly discovered a blue envelope on the desk, opened it up. It was—

'Why is it that you don't put seeing me on your work schedule! Come see me once! I will wait for you at the campus gate.' I had no way of resisting such a stubborn and cheeky, cute and childish turn of phrase. I put on my coat, took a strong drag of a Chi Szu brand cigarette, walked to the campus gate. She was already there. At this time it was suitable to take a stroll down a quiet tarmac road, passing fields of wheat, several desolate graves, faraway villages buried in wheat, and a murder of crows flying across the sky . . .

'You really love to smoke.'

'Lonely men take cigarettes as their lovers. It comes to visit me when I'm lonesome, in the car, on the bed, when I'm meditating, when I'm fatigued . . . even when I'm in the bath, it will come. Some might say that it doesn't understand etiquette, but we are old friends . . . '

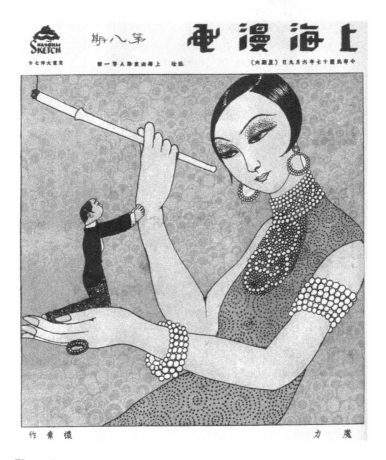

Figure 4

Huaisu, 'Fascination'. *Shanghai manhua* 8 (9 June 1928), front cover (http://mclc.osu.edu/rc/pubs/laing.htm).

'Every day I'm surrounded by beer-swilling men. Bumping into somebody fresh like you really stimulates my appetite.'

Yikes, she takes me as a stimulant.

'Then your stomach is not healthy.'

'That's because men have harmed me. Their cowardice, their ignorance, the rat-like look in their eyes, the pretence of sadness in their faces . . . it all gives me a case of indigestion.'

'That can only be blamed on the snacks that girls like to eat, you take Nestlé chocolates, **Sunkist**, Shanghai Beer, candied walnuts, peanuts and other stuff and swallow it all down at once, so of course you're going to have some severe digestion problems. All of the chocolates, **Sunkist** and other stuff that goes through your system . . . how can it not wear a sad face?'

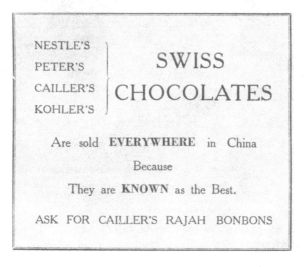

Figure 5

Swiss chocolates advertisement, *North-China Daily News*, 3 November 1924.

'That's why I want to eat stimulating food!'

'Stimulating food doesn't go down easy for a person with digestion problems.'

'Ah, whatever!'

'Have a lot of men passed through your digestive system?'

'I'm suffering from constipation, I want to push them out of my system, but I can't, it's really a tough predicament. They all wear their hearts on their sleeves, putting on their pathetic clown masks . . . I can only treat them all as fools and that's it.'

(Danger—will I not also be swallowed by her like a chocolate, only to come out the other end as a waste product? But then again, she's just as forthright as me! I'm looking at her red bean-like mouth—will this mouth tell lies?) Thus did I doubt her. She crouched on the side of the path and picked a purple wildflower, and stuck it onto my shirt. 'Do you know the name of this flower?'

'Tell me.'

'It's called **Forget-me-not**,' and she smiled brightly.

Heavens! I was worrying again. I was already in her mouth, being treated like a chocolate bonbon! I felt the virus of misogyny spreading into my veins. I didn't dare to look at her head leaning ever so slightly, walked forward and came to sit on a patch of grass. On the lawn was a leaning slope, and atop it a willow tree grew, I lay down under the willow branches, watching the shadows flit across our bodies, while Rongzi sat there playing with a stalk of grass.

'A sufferer of misogyny, you are!'

From amid the smoke of the Chi Szu brand cigarette, I saw her arrogant nose, eyes that were laughing at me, and disappointed lips.

'Tell me, from where does your virus come?'

'It was a present given to me by a girl who tells lies.'

'So you're spreading your virus in a magazine? What a truly hateful person!'

'The virus that I carry is the only cure for girls who have indigestion problems.'

'You really don't make girls detest you!'

'Let me read a poem for you—' I read a small poem by **Louise Gilmore**:

> *If I were a peacock,*
> *I would have a thousand eyes*
> *To see you.*
> *If I were a centipede,*
> *I would have a hundred feet*
> *To follow you.*
> *If I were an octopus*
> *I would have eight arms*
> *To embrace you.*
> *If I were a cat*
> *I would have nine lives*
> *To love you.*
> *If I were God*
> *I would have three bodies*
> *To give you.*

She didn't make a sound, but I could see that she was thinking, what a detestable guy! She just pretended not to understand anything, but now she was at it again.

'Let's go back.'

'Why do you want to leave now?'

'Men are all fools,' she said angrily.

I accompanied her back down the tarmac road now enshrouded by the twilight. For several days after, when I returned from the tennis court carrying my tennis racquet and went into a restaurant to fill my stomach with some afternoon tea, and lazily strolled back towards my dorm, stopping for five minutes to rest on the grass and waiting for dinner, and when I was ambling from the classroom to the sports ground with a book under my arm, I'd often see her, either running from the dorm to the school gate to catch the bus, or from there walking back to her dorm. When I saw her, she'd just casually say hello, and there were no letters from her.

But that evening, I was about to go to the library, when a letter arrived:

'Come over here one more time—understand?' in this commanding tone. Once again I had to go there! Was it not good just to forget it? I felt that I was standing next to dangerous deep waters, but, in the end, I ran over there.

The moon had emerged, over there, in the corner of an imperial dorm, dark red, like a great big basin. Casting the moon behind me, I walked with her out of the school gates, walking along the tarmac road. The road seemed to stretch into the horizon, and suddenly the headlights of a car came streaming at us from the horizon. It lit up a billboard at the road's edge showing a lady smoking Chi Szu brand cigarettes and smiling happily, and then it disappeared again. We walked to a bridge, and stood leaning against the railing. I blew some smoke towards the moon.

'Has your indigestion problem improved recently?'

'It's been a bit better, but today it flared up again.'

'So you have need of a stimulant again?'

She smiled from within the cloud of Chi Szu brand cigarette smoke.

'Let me recite a poem for you.'

She faced the moon, her waist leaning against the railing. I watched her shadow, cast into the water.

If I were a peacock,
I would have a thousand eyes
To see you.
If I were a centipede,
I would have a hundred feet
To follow you.
If I were . . .

I grabbed her hand. She lifted up her head, and closed her eyes—in the silvery light of the moon, her eyelids were purple. I kissed her flowery lips, it was like drinking wine, lightly lightly sipping wine. And then—'You wouldn't take advantage of me, would you!'—smiling.

The moon shone on our backs, the Chi Szu brand cigarette fell into the water, like a meteorite, while beneath my eyes I discovered a pair of black jade eyeballs.

'I fell in love with you the first time I saw you!' She put her lovely head into my arms, giggling. 'It's only you who I am searching for! What a lovely masculine face you have, such a strong jawline, so modern looking . . . such gentle eyes, a knowing mouth . . .'

I let that lying mouth of hers spill forth words like frothy beer foam.

'This mouth may not be telling the truth.' At the dorm, I thought this again. From the window upstairs somebody was blowing on a **Saxophone**. The spring breeze blew on my face, curling up my collar.

"Heavens! Heavens!"

The next day I thought about it for a bit, and felt that I was on dangerous ground. She was a dangerous animal, but I wasn't a good hunter. Had I captured her now? Or was I being captured by her? My anxiety was growing as I pondered this unsolvable puzzle. In the evening I received a letter from her, which innocently went: "You are truly a despicable person! I thought that you would come see me today, who could have guessed you didn't come after all? You are already my captive, why are you still fighting me off? . . ." I didn't dare read any further—wasn't the message very clear already? I couldn't be her captive. I threw the letter on the table, and retreated into a city of books, a mountain of manuscripts, and a river of black ink.

But, alas! I felt that every letter O was the imprint of her lips; the eyes in the poster of **Vilma Banky** on the wall looked like her eyes, **Nancy Carrol**'s smile looked like her smile, and strangely her nose was growing on **Norma Shearer**'s face. Her lips were blossoming on the tip of my pen, on the bald pate of Tolstoy, on the manuscripts . . . on the rose-patterned lampshade . . . I picked up the letter and continued to read: "Are you afraid of me? Are you as cowardly as the other men? This evening's moon appears to be wearing a layer of fog as it creeps over the willow branches. Yet I miss your lovely face—on a two-dimensional surface, the lines jump straight out constructing a three-dimensional image, it's a miracle!" Such stimulating, creative sentences.

One more visit, for the sake of such lovely sentences. The Clara Bow-like words and creative sentences surrounded me, hand in hand they danced the Black Bottom, pulling me to the door—they could pull the entire male race over there.

Sitting on the stone steps, hand supporting her chin, head askant, quietly singing a nocturne to the roses, there was Rongzi, in the shimmering light of the door lamp, her dove-like shadow drawn on the ground, leaping from the darkness into the light. She smiled and skipped over to me.

"Don't you want to escape from my clutches? Why did you come here again?"

"Aren't you waiting for me?"

"I was bored, so I'm sitting here watching the night view."

"Did you not just put some new Tangee lipstick on your lips?"

"You're despicable!"

She took me by the arm and we walked into the darkness of the sports ground. We walked from the light into the line between light and shadow, then into the darkness, where we stopped. She looked at me as if asking, "You have forgotten."

"Rongzi, you love me, don't you?"

"Yes."

This "mouth" doesn't tell lies. I kissed her mouth that didn't tell lies.

"Rongzi, what about those playthings?"

Figure 6

Tangee cosmetics advertisement, *North-China Daily News*, 17 June 1928.

"Playthings are just playthings, and that's it."

"When you're with those playthings, don't you say you love them too?"

"That's all because men are so stupid, if you don't tell them, they'll follow you around like beggars making pleading, grumpy, hateful, and cajoling faces . . . when you meet with beggars who won't let you be, don't you have to give them a copper?"

Perhaps she was including me as one of her playthings. I lowered my head.

"Actually you don't have to tell someone you love them or not, you just know what's in the other's heart. I love you. Do you believe me? Yes—believe me? Tell me! I know you believe me."

I looked at her cheating, lying mouth and knew well that she was telling a lie, but I believed her lie anyhow.

High-speed love! I loved her, but she was still a stranger to me. I didn't understand her, her thoughts, soul, interests were things I didn't comprehend. We hadn't established a basis for friendship, but love was already being built up without any firm foundation.

Every night, I'd always whistle a cuckoo sound at her window. She'd always jump out like a child, quietly singing a nocturne, and go to the door of the dormitory shouting, '**Alexy**.' I would play a tune on the mouth harp and she would come. From the shimmering light came the shadows of plants, she would grasp the collar of my **Coat**, as if to say, 'You've forgotten again,' waiting for me to kiss her. I gave her a light kiss, and then—'You won't treat me like a plaything again,' I thought, but it wasn't as if I stuck to her like a beggar, she was sticking to me. After that, she hung herself like a cane on my arm, and strolled around with the corners of her skirt floating. I took pains to build a foundation of friendship underneath the love.

'Have you read *La Dame aux Camelias*?'

'This is something our grandparents should have read.'

'So do you like to read works of social realism, like Zola's *Nana*, or Dostoevsky's *Crime and Punishment*?'

'When I want to go to sleep I pick them up and read them, since for me they are just like sleep-inducing medicine. I enjoy reading Paul Morand, Yokomitsu Riichi, Horiguchi Daigaku, and Sinclair Lewis—I especially love Lewis.'

'What about our own country?'

'I like Liu Na'ou's new speech skills, Guo Jianying's comics, and your violent prose and wild flavour . . .'

This was truly a girl who lived on stimulation and speed, Rongzi! **Jazz**, machines, speed, urban culture, American flavour, contemporary beauty . . . she was made up of all these things.

'Have you been cured of your misogyny yet?'

'Yes. How about your indigestion?'

'Much better, since I stopped eating so many snacks.'

'A new discovery for 1931: the virus of misogyny is a very effective cure for stomach illness.'

'But maybe it's the other way around, the by-products of indigestion are also effective at treating misogyny.'

Correct—this was precisely the problem. To put it another way, in relation to this dangerous animal, was I a good hunter, or simply an unlucky lamb?

Truly, going to see her had become part of my work schedule—but sometimes I was too lazy to do my other work.

Every night, I'd sit by the pond on campus, listening to the lies she told in her Suzhou-style words, and I'd believe these lies. Watching the shadows on the water's surface, faintly blowing a tune on my mouth harp, it was just like a dream. She'd count the stars like a child, one, two, three . . . I'd kiss her flower-like mouth once, twice, three times . . .

'What loneliness is there in life? What pain?'

The Chi Szu brand cigarette smoke was dancing, mixed together with the moonlight. She was leaning on my shoulder, singing 'Kiss me again', and I kissed her, fourth time, fifth time, sixth time . . .

Thus, going to see her became a part of my life. Bathing, exercise, studying, sleeping, eating, and then going to see her framed my whole life—life isn't something you can change so easily.

Yet how could one maintain such lofty heights of love? At this speed, one could have circled around the earth three times. If the high speed of this love were to slow down, it would lose its stimulation, and then wouldn't Rongzi, who lived on stimulation, discard it? And would she not then discard me? Then she would go on manipulating her playthings! She still hadn't cleansed her system of the faeces of those playthings! Having solved this puzzle, it was truly a tragedy—when I thought through these things, there was nothing I could do, so one night I wrote a letter to her—

> You cured me of misogyny but you gave me a case
> of nervous anxiety instead. Meeting such a fast girl
> as you! Falling in love this quickly, would you not
> abandon me just as quickly? Thinking about this,
> I'm very worried. Tell me, Rongzi, will there be a day
> when you stop loving me?

I really suffered from weak nerves syndrome. But, her return letter arrived: 'Come tomorrow night, I will tell you.' This was the tone that I used to use with her. Nestlé chocolate, **Sunkist**, Shanghai beer, candied chestnuts . . . I hoped that I wasn't this sort of thing.

The next afternoon I thought about these things, and for some unknowable reason I was depressed. I ran over to see Rongzi, but she wasn't there. Ten thousand tonnes weighed upon my heart. How after all did I come to care for her that much! Returning to the dorm, there was nobody in the room, outside the window on the sports ground a lonely dog was lying there, my wool hat cast a seductive glance at me. I wore it, and followed **XX** Road walking towards a flower garden run by a Russian. I felt like I was missing something, missing a girl accompanying me. Treating a girl as a cane while walking—at least it was a bit more convenient.

Underneath the willow branches, I slowly rowed a boat, singing 'Rio Rita' in low tones—this was a good way of passing the time. On the shore stood a Russian in charge of the village, slowly drinking vodka, smoking strong Russian cigarettes, looking at me. On the river were two white swans, lying on the surface, all around the swans were rippling rings of water. The water was reflecting trees, blue sky, white clouds, and suddenly a goat appeared. I looked back and saw it eating grass on the water's edge, looking at the sky. Letting the boat follow the river's current was like floating to the edge of the sky.

A lovely voice could now be heard, singing the *Minuet in G* in a high soprano. It seemed to be coming from atop the water, and rippled between the water and the mist. But I recognized that singing voice, it was coming from the mouth that told lies. It slowly came towards me, and I could hear the sound of rowing. I sat up— Heavens! It was Rongzi leaning on another man's shoulder. The man had a dreamy gaze, and he was looking my way. Closer, closer, the boat brushed past.

'Alexy!'

She called me in this way, and waved at me; a white silk scarf was wrapped around her shoulders, the wind was blowing it back and it was fluttering, and the corner of the fluttering scarf exposed her smile. I didn't answer, and I felt the virus of misogyny once again activating in my veins. I pulled on the oars vigorously, unwilling to turn my head, and collapsed onto the floor of the boat. Flow, water! Flow, flow to a place where a mouth didn't tell lies, flow to a place where there was no flower-like mouth, flow to a place where there was no cheating mouth! Flow, flow to the edge of the sky, flow to a place without people, flow to the kingdom of dreams, flow to a place that I don't know . . . but, from behind me was the call of a cuckoo! From amid the white clouds came the head of a cat, a laughing gentle face, the white scarf floating on her hair like music.

I had just sat up halfway, and the crabapple-coloured high heels had already crossed over me. Rongzi was sitting by my side, hanging over my shoulder like a little bird. When I sat up, I saw the man in the other boat had a shocked expression on his face, and slowly he lost his smile and replaced it with a depressed look.

'Rongzi.'

'Off you go.'

He sat there frozen in shock for a spell, then rowed his boat away. His figure retreated in the distance, but his depressed voice could be heard singing, 'I belong to a girl who belongs to somebody else,' floating over lightly on the waves.

'Fool!'

'. . .'

'What?'

'. . .'

Suddenly she erupted in peals of laughter like silver bells.

'What's the matter?'

'Take a look at your face in the water—what an angry-looking face!'

I also laughed—when coming across such a person, there is no other way.

'Rongzi, don't you just love me alone?'

'Aren't I loving you?'

'What about that man just now?'

'Isn't that just a chocolate?'

Thinking about her jumping from his boat onto mine, thinking about the face that looked like it was passing too much chocolate out of its system . . .

'But, Rongzi, will there be a day when you don't love me any more?'

She rested her head on my shoulder, and in a sighing voice said:

'Will there be a day when I don't love you?'

She lifted her head and stroked my hair, and once again I believed her lies.

On the road back, I was happy—finally I was not a plaything!

After three days, a new desire began to sprout in my heart. I would cure her of constipation. I didn't want her to tell her waste materials that she loved them. If she didn't listen to me, then she didn't love me alone, and thus it was best to forget about her. If things went on this way, my weak nerves syndrome would cause even more damage—and, having made such decision, that evening I said to Rongzi:

'Expel that waste matter!'

'And what else?'

'Don't go out all the time!'

'And what else?' She suddenly laughed.

'What do you mean?'

'You have also turned into a fool!'

Hearing that laughter, I immediately grew angry. I cast a baleful glance at her, and made up my mind to leave her. She simply treated me as a child! She caught up to me and held me back, she raised her head a little, those eyes like black jade, the long lashes . . . she wrapped her arms around my neck:

'Do you hate me?'

She stared at me as if she was afraid to lose something.

'No, Rongzi.'

Rongzi was standing on her tiptoes—it was like holding a cat, that kind of touch. Her speech was a *double entendre*, it made you realize it was a lie, it also made you believe that lie. In front of her I felt like a target that had been hit by a bull's-eye, lying stiff. What way was there to resist her! But looking at it from the surface, it seemed as if she had been conquered by me, this dangerous yet lovable animal. The pride of thinking myself a great hunter delighted me.

For two weeks, Rongzi didn't go out. Before me she curled up like a kitten, who in winter would crouch upon the rug in front of the fireplace. I was surprised by her gentle compliance. On the weekend, she would just hang around the campus, bringing her radio, and going on picnics with me. She would lie on the soft grass, and in the late spring breeze she would sing. In the fields of wild wheat, she would run around like a child. Sitting atop a grave mound, we would watch the sun slip below the horizon, listening to the call of cuckoos in the fields, laughing, pointing at the spires of a faraway cathedral, leaning on me . . . I was happy. I loved her, with gentle hands, delicate smiles, and all the heart of a twenty-year-old youth.

Yet there will come a day when a great hunter is defeated by a wild beast.

On Saturday afternoon she sent a letter:

> Today I must attend a Party. Don't go out; I will return tonight—I know that if you want to go out, you would

go to a dance hall, but I do not wish to know that you
are embracing another girl.

That evening I gave a cuckoo's call in front of her window. A gale
of laughter riding upon the crimson light escaped out from the
curtains. I waited for half an hour but did not hear the singing of a
nocturne or the sound of 'Alexy'. I understood that she was out. Like
beer, like peanuts, like chocolate candies, like **Sunkist** . . . those
faces of male playthings, one by one, floated into my reverie. I
walked over to the bridge by the campus gate thinking that I'd wait
for her there, and get a good look at the man who escorted her
back—the boldness of a man who escorted his female companion
back in a car at night, I understood well.

The four lamps on the bridge, their dim yellow light floated
on the surface of the water, as I sat there quietly. One by one, cars
drove past on the road, their lights shining on the trees and casting
shadows, only to pass by. None of them took a turn and headed
into the campus, in the end, all of the lovers walking in the night
entered the campus; they all knew me, and their surprised eyes
shone pair by pair as they passed me. From the window of the
dorm a **Saxophone** charged me—

I opened my mouth wide and yelled: 'When one is lovable,
love one! Women's hearts, like the plum rains, are unpredictable—'
Thinking of Rongzi in another man's embrace, I felt as if my heart
had been dug out. When all the lights on campus had gone out,
treading on the desolate moonlight, like the rustling of leaves in
the autumn wind, I walked back alone, dejected . . .

On Sunday morning I ate breakfast, while I was reading the
illustrated section of the newspaper *Shenbao*. A friend who had
not had enough sleep entered the campus, and, regarding me with

eyes that had imbibed too many **Cocktail**[s], with legs that were still waltzing, he smiled and said:

'Last night Rongzi was at the Paris dance hall, dancing like mad—Oh, sorry, all around her were many men like weeds floating on a pond, each of them would kill to have her in his arms.'

At around 5 p.m. another letter arrived from Rongzi. I put my fate in my hands and read:

> It couldn't be helped, last night after the Party, it was too late, I couldn't return. I will definitely come back tonight, wait for me.

I stood at the campus gate waiting until the last bus entered the campus, and still she wasn't on it. I decided to go to Shanghai with my friends. The rough road shook the car around, the car tossed my body about like a suitcase, my body jangled my nerves—thinking about bumping into her in a dance hall, I felt an acute case of nervous disorder.

First I went to the Paris Dance Hall but she wasn't there. Through the **Jazz** forest of dancing legs, amid the oceanic laughter, I undertook a pilgrimage into the dance halls, but she still wasn't there. I returned to the Paris, and lost my soul dancing until 11 p.m., when I saw her enter, dressed to the max, trailing a load of chocolate candy-like men in her wake.

At that point my foot trod on the shoe of a dancer, and I even bumped into her. I sat there dejectedly, thinking about how to deal with the situation. Rongzi was sitting at a table not far from us. I sat with my back to her, lifting my glass of liquor and anaesthetizing myself. I danced a quickstep, and, in front of her, I planted a passionate kiss on the dancer I was with. The liquor turned my eyes red, and I became a man without feelings. Back at my table, the waiter brought over a piece of paper, and placed an apple on top of it:

> Why are you making such a big fuss out of this? You are such a fool! Eat this apple and cool down your nerves. Looking at your wild eyes pains me.

I turned my head, and saw two jade-black eyes staring at me with deep emotion. I rested my chin on the glass and was preparing to lash her with a scolding. The melody of a fox-trot was floating on the shiny surface of the dance floor.

'Alexy!'

She danced over to the edge of my table. I quickly stood up straight.

'Go to hell, cheating mouth, lying mouth!'

'Buddy, this is not the attitude of a **Gentleman**. Look at yourself, you look like an angry bear . . .' said the man dancing with her, making fun of me with a funny face.

'Buzz off, you son of a bitch, this is none of your business!'

'Yuh.' *Pah*! I received a slap on the cheek.

'Say, what's the big idea?'

'No, Alexy, say no, by golly!' Rongzi held me back by the arms. I pushed her away.

'You don't mean . . .'

'I mean it.'

I let go with a punch, and the man collapsed onto the floor. Rongzi looked at the man who had hit a man on her behalf, but maintained a poker face revealing no emotion, and sat at the edge of the table. My friends pulled me out of there. I was yelling, 'I'm through!' but I felt like a criminal who had perpetrated a foolish deed.

For three days in a row, I stayed at home by the bedside writing Strindberg dialogue, reading essays that mocked women, fiercely proclaiming patriarchy . . .

'Forget her! Forget her!'

But could I forget this lying girl, Rongzi? If Rongzi had not told lies, I would have forgotten her long ago. Living on the same campus I could not help but see this lying mouth every day. To me there was a cold look on her face—and for a week she did not pay any attention to me. But she still had that lovely pair of dancing feet treading on rosy red high heels, the colour of crabapple blossoms; the bottom corners of her *qipao* fluttering, as if standing in a light breeze, wearing a long red silk *qipao*; an animal that was a mixture of gentleness and danger, with a cat's head, and a snake's body . . .

On Monday while I was attending the weekly ceremony, I stood at the very back of the hall, and didn't dare look forward, fearing I would bump into her. She came as well and also stood at the very back of the hall as if nothing had happened, chuckling to herself. I put on an upset face, and gave her an entreating look. The two arms that were sticking out of a short-sleeved shirt had once climbed up my collar. She turned around to look at my face—she was about to smile, but I was about to cry. The schoolmates looked at me, and asked me, what's the matter, and then they looked at her and asked her. Everybody was staring at me, so I left in the middle of the ceremony and ran out.

The next class was modern history, my seat was next to hers. The teacher with his glasses and slumped left shoulder was famous for his research on the Industrial Revolution. That day we had just reached this chapter. The speed of my pencil kept up with the pace of the teacher's saliva spurting out of his mouth as he lectured. All that I wrote on the paper was—'that cheating mouth, that cheating mouth'.

She laughed.

'Rongzi!'

Her red lips looked like a shut clam. I wrote on the paper: 'You have a lying mouth, but I am willing to believe your lies! Can you let me listen to your lovely lies?' And I gave it to her.

'After class go to the lawn of XX Road and wait for me.'

She went back to her notebook and paid no more attention to me.

After class I went there and waited for her. It was already summer, the wheat had grown up to the hips, golden yellow, and very deep. Sun lit up the entire landscape on the wild field, and from somewhere came the calls of cuckoos, crying out the April countryside. I sat there like a convicted killer awaiting his death sentence, as I waited for her to arrive. Time froze, and for a long time I waited in vain. The sound of the campus bell came wafting over and reverberated in the wheat field, and then melted into the smoke from the kitchen fires of the nearby village. Presently, Rongzi came flying in like a pigeon, clothed in white silk pyjamas, her hair streaming out from a white silk knot dancing a tango, reminding me of a water lily.

'That day you were unwilling to watch me dancing with that other man, right?'

Confronting me so directly with the cause of my guilt, she gave me no option but to admit to my crime. I lifted my head and looked at this judge standing there in such radiance, and my eyes begged her for mercy.

'But can you really interfere in these affairs? Why do so in such a foolish way? If your words make sense to me of course I will listen to you, but if they don't, how can you make me obey you? Don't you know, the past few days you acted too foolishly, so I didn't pay any attention to you. Today you seem to have calmed down—remember . . .' She recited the terms of the sentence, and I knelt down on the ground and kissed her feet.

She also sat down, placed my head on her legs, and brushed my hair back with her hand, saying quietly, 'Remember, I love you, child. But you cannot interfere in my activities.' Then she kissed me lightly. I closed my eyes and smiled—'Rongzi'—so saying, I felt happy, but this happiness was the product of having been pardoned for my crime. After all that, I had become her captive animal!

'Do you really think that a woman can only be worshipped by one man? As for love, one can only love one other person, but as for playthings and tools, there can be many of these. Don't tell me that you don't have photos of other ladies in your pocket.'

'Ah, Rongzi.'

From that day onward, she was worshipped by many other men, and, as for me, I was as happy as a lamb loved by a lion. I had lost my resistance. In the end, she limited the number of times I could leave the campus, and if I did leave I had to return by 9 p.m. and give a cuckoo's call at her window as a report—could I not be willing to accept this sort of limitation? No, at 8.30 p.m. I would hurry back in a forty-mile-per-hour car and report in front of her window, and this sort of fidelity brought me happiness. But she even went so far as to limit the kisses I could give her. Still, for a lamb facing a lion, what could one think about such things, although I was willing to trade a drop of blood for one flowery kiss.

I recall one evening, she was returning from a worship session off campus, wearing a purple wool *qipao*—in terms of her attire she was becoming more and more of an expert. In contrast to other girls who only wore silk garments, which made them look like eels, she knew how to wear fabrics that gave you a gentle feel. As usual she was the Rongzi who sang nocturnes, while walking like a cloud. Under the silvery moonlight, she looked like a silver-purple-winged night butterfly, flapping her wings sedately, bringing the April breeze, the scent of love, and golden dreams. I held firmly this big night butterfly, thinking to swallow her lips covered with dark red Tangee lipstick. She pulled a violet from her hair and stuck it into my mouth, and then this big night butterfly flew away from my arms. Holding the flower in my mouth, I watched her fly away, the soles of two high-heeled shoes dancing in the nightscape, mixed with the sound of her laughter. When I seized her again, she hid herself in my arms smiling, and I had no way of kissing her.

'Rongzi, one flowery kiss, a purple kiss.'

'Purple kisses are for children who aren't greedy.'

I fooled her, forced her, begged her, and lured her, but she still hid in my arms. More clever than a mouse. She was in my arms but did not let me kiss her, it wasn't an easy matter. So did the time pass.

'Rongzi, if I successfully win a kiss from you, then you have to kiss me three times every night.'

'Sure, but this week you will not succeed. Before the break you may not kiss me, and, furthermore, every day you must say one hundred flattering sentences about me, each one must be fresh and different.'

This was a war even more ferocious than the Great War, three kisses a day, otherwise, one hundred flattering phrases per day, each one new and different. Before deciding upon the strategy I had already boldly declared war. After she left, there lingered a sensuous and warm scent, floating around me, this was the subtle substance produced by our loving touches. Within this space imbricated with the scent of love, I awaited another night to deliver her back into my arms. However, the next night came, and I did not speak these words. For the following three days, I did not go see her. On the fourth day, I grabbed her hand, put on a worried face, my eyes full of vitriol. Two giant tears fell from my eyes.

'Rongzi!' I felt like I was in a play.

'What the matter today, it seems like you are depressed?'

'How do I put it, it's something I could not have conceived. I cannot love you anymore! Give me a kiss, one last kiss!' My heat was jumping, in one moment victory or failure would be decided.

Her arms embraced my neck, kissing me; suddenly, her black jade eyes shone and she smiled. On her tiptoes she kissed me once, twice, three times.

'Clever child!'

So the next week I ate purple Tangee every night and had fulfilling conversations. But her lips became colder every night, even though the weather became hotter and hotter. As the summer break approached, my heart shrank as the exam results were posted on the public announcement board.

'Rongzi, have you gradually stopped loving me?'

'Fool!'

This kind of matter need not be asked about, an old practised hand would not wish that women told the truth. And even if you asked, would they tell you? Fool! Was I not her plaything? But every night we kissed.

There were more and more parties that she wished to attend. And gradually I spent less and less time with her. I was depressed. I often heard others report that she had been out playing with so-and-so, and where she had been with so-and-so. With such a sad face, schoolmates thought that I was nervous about the upcoming exams—who knew that I wanted this exam period to stretch as long as it could be sustained? Thinking about the coming break, I was stripped of the power to even study.

'It's simply that I come from a wealthy family so I must bear many pains. I cannot decide anything, I cannot even keep a lover. In Shanghai, I am supervised by men sent by my father, just as if they are supervising somebody's property and status. Heavens! He's busy finding a matchmaker for me. Every week they always send me two or three photos of bald-headed men smiling above thick ties. In my room I can show you more photos than the number of cosmetics I own. I have two elder brothers, and every time they see me they bring a Ph.D. or a master's degree holder. They are all middle-aged men with clean-shaven faces. They are all disdainful: one man took me to a municipal hall to listen to music, and he did not shave, and he teased me saying, "While I was waiting for you to make yourself up, it grew out again."'

'So why don't you get engaged? PhDs, MAs, professors, aren't there so many opportunities?'

'It is because I am only willing to treat them as playthings. Recently things haven't been right, Daddy only wants to marry me off, like he was clearing his inventory. Does he not really love me? I really don't understand why he has to marry off the daughter he loves so much. Wouldn't it be better to keep him company for the rest of his life? I greatly fear marrying—husband, child, household—that would really take away my youth. Why should I marry? But now I have no way out, Daddy is forcing me, he's saying if I don't listen to him, then next semester he won't let me come over to Shanghai and study. If I marry, I will have to choose an extremely ugly and stupid person to be my husband, clever husbands cannot be manipulated by their wives. When I'm happy to love him, I will love him, and when I don't feel like loving him, I won't let him touch me. A cute lover, an ugly husband, and playthings that are not annoying—arranging life this way might not be too lonely?'

'Do you want to get engaged?'

Rongzi did not say anything, she bit her lower lip and softly sang a nocturne, but, suddenly, tears started falling, like pearls, one, two . . .

'Don't you?'

I kept asking her.

'Yes, with a banker's son—he adores me so. If he can just grab my feet and be my husband, he will be satisfied. That little fatty. For our engagement party, what do you plan to give me as a gift?'

At that point the line of our conversation was cut off. Depression and doubt, contemplation and sadness . . . all of these were mixed up in my brain like a cocktail.

Rongzi stood in the moonlight.

'What I just told you was a lie. I've been engaged for a while now. My fiancé is in America, and he's coming back this summer; he is a very strong man, when he was in China, he led the school soccer team, at that time, he would pat me on the head and call me little sister, but when he returns, I will introduce you to him.'

'So you've long since been engaged?'

'What of it? Does that make you angry? I'm fooling you, I haven't been engaged, and don't wish to be. Look at your shocked face! If you take what a girl says at any moment as the truth, you will certainly go crazy, eh?'

'I've long since gone crazy. Look, like this . . .'

I suddenly ran away without looking backward.

After completing the exams, she became ill.

The doctor told her it was from eating too much candy—her stomach was weak and could not digest properly. Fearing that she would be lonely, I rode my bike in the June sun ten miles to **XX** University to bring her girlfriend over to see her. I went to Shanghai to buy her a bunch of carnations to put by her bedside. After eating, I went to the front of her dorm and stood there, with my head empty. I didn't dare speak a word. The sun was shining on top of my head, the sun was shining on my face, the sun moved to the base of the wall, the sun shone into the back of the room, the sun sank down below the field of shorn wheat. I watched Rongzi sleeping behind white lace curtains, and I forgot all about my own body drenched in sweat.

I dreamed about Rongzi, fearing that her black jade eyes were shrivelling away with illness.

The next day I ran over to see her—her school mates had all left the room. The blankets on the bed were in disarray, the white carnations were all drooping their heads in loneliness, but I could not find those familiar eyes, or the voice that used to call me Alexy. I asked the aunty at the door, who told me that her father had come to take her away, and I feared that I might not see her again.

I lingered outside her window half the day, as the rain drizzled down desolately.

In the rain, slowly, falling leaves making sounds like crickets, I made my way back home. Cars filled to the brim with luggage and people made their way out of the campus gates in a long parade. In the desolate sports ground, drifting, drifting, that long, long tarmac road, the ancient copper-coloured lamps, the pond with floating algae, the vast field—here lay buried my love, Rongzi's smile.

In the evening she returned.

'Tomorrow I'm going home. I've come to pack my luggage.'

I did not speak. I waited at my place, and when I went to the women's dorm the door was locked, so I stood outside her window. It was raining, and I just stood in the rain. She had really lost weight, and her eyes looked depressed.

'Rongzi, why are you depressed?'

'Why bother to ask?'

'Tell me, Rongzi, I feel that lately you no longer love me. Do you still love me after all?'

'But why do you bother asking this?'

A few moments passed.

'Do you still love me? Will you always love me?'

'Yes, Rongzi, with all my heart.'

She put her arms through the steel window bars and hugged my neck, kissing me. 'So love me forever.' Then she quietly lowered her head.

On the way back home, I finally realized that my back was slick with rain, and that I hadn't eaten all evening.

The next morning I bumped into Rongzi at the stone stage of the classroom.

'Goodbye!'

'Goodbye!'

Then she left, like falling leaves in autumn, in a light drizzle slanted by the wind, under a blue oil-paper umbrella, treading step by step in her lovely crimson high-heeled shoes. Turning back her head, she gave me a glance as if she wished to say something, and then softly, softly, she sang a nocturne, and vanished into the willow trees.

I stood there, and the light rain brought me anxiety.

After half a day, I ran in front of her window, all of the girls had already left the dorm. There was an empty bed in the room, and a bare table. On the walls hung the photo of Clara Bow smiling in her loneliness, and the carnations now lay upon the floor. The call of a cuckoo came from the wheat-shorn field. I copied it, and this lonely cry resounded in the room, and then receded.

On the tarmac road in the light June rain I shuffled out, turning my head back. The willows were now mixed together with the twilight. I played the tune 'Souvenir' on my mouth harp, and caught the last bus to Shanghai.

I wrote eight letters, but did not get one in reply. On the road, making wild eyes, I stared at every girl dressed in red, and with my heart jumping out of my mouth I followed them staring, but it was not her! In the dance halls, I sat there quietly, watching the dancers' feet, searching for that pair of feet sporting crimson high heels, those lovely feet. I watched every pair of feet stomping, but, but it was not her! It was not her! I went to Rio Rita Village, on the river, slowly rowing a boat, listening to all the sounds of songs floating on the water's surface, wishing to hear that soft nocturne melody. But she wasn't there! She wasn't there! At the banquet, looking at all the eyes, wishing to find those familiar black eyes that seemed to hide Eastern secrets; each eye, brown eye, eyes with long lashes, eyes that spoke, were all shocked before my searching eyes. But it wasn't her! It wasn't her! At home, every time one o'clock rolled around, I would look at the letterbox, every letter I received worried me, I wished to find those waltzing, Clara Bow-like letters. But it wasn't her! It wasn't her! Every time I heard somebody call my name, I pricked my ears like a wolf, wishing to hear that wistful sound of

'Alexy'. But it wasn't her! It wasn't her! Everywhere I searched for a mouth that told such flowery lies. But it wasn't her! It wasn't her . . .

She once told me that she might move in with her aunt, and her aunt lived on Bubbling Well Road, she even told me the address. In the end, I decided to go look for her, perhaps I would be scolded by her aunt, perhaps even driven out, but I only wished to see my Rongzi once more. In the June sun, I walked from Jing'an Temple to the Race Course, and then walked back again, then walked over here, then walked over there. There was no such address at all. In the June sun, I walked for four or five days, and then fell ill.

In the throes of my illness—'maybe she isn't in Shanghai'. Thus I consoled myself.

Old Liao, a friend who had graduated, was returning to Sichuan, and I went to the ship to see him off.

'Last night I saw Rongzi dancing with a man who wasn't you at the Paris . . .'

I heard a crashing sound from inside the intricate structure of my brain. Later, another friend whom I was sending off told me a similar story. They were all my good friends, and they all knew me well.

'Forget her! After all, it's regret!'

Listening to their words of advice, I smiled a bitter smile that forced out all the waste products of chocolate candy. Old Liao played the guitar, while the waters of the Huangpu River looked like golden fish-scales under the moonlight. I made a song.

'I am a plaything after all!'

While returning home, my twenty-year-old heart was full of sorrow.

'A lonely man ought to simply buy a cane.'

The next day, I bought a cane. It accompanied me, along with Chi Szu brand cigarettes, the whole day, as step by step I strolled upon the road of life.

2

Five in a Nightclub
夜總會裡的五個人 (1933)

'Five in a Nightclub' takes place on one specific day and night: Saturday, 6 April 1932. This story, which complements Mu's more famous 'Shanghai Fox-trot', is both a paean to the glamorous and energetic environment of the modern metropolis and a trenchant critique of modern urban life. Mu begins the story with five brief vignettes of seemingly unrelated characters, each on his or her own downward trajectory. Each character is faced with a difficult problem or situation which appears unresolvable. The situations thrust upon the characters are reflective of the rapid pace of urban life and its ever-shifting trends and vicissitudes. The female character, Daisy, confronts the fact of her aging, and the loss of her youthful beauty. Another character has just lost his fortune through speculation (one discerns the spectre of Mu's own father in this man). Yet another has been summarily dismissed from his post in the mayor's office.

Following these short vignettes, Mu takes us into the space of a Shanghai nightclub, where the 'primitive African' music of jazz assaults the senses. Within that space, Mu deftly brings together the five characters, whose lives are now connected through their common desire to find temporary escape from their sorrows by throwing themselves into the city's famed nightlife. Within this milieu, the five characters play out their fates.

We find that the nightclub is a 'see and be seen' space, where people parade themselves ostentatiously while constantly sizing up the other guests. In one brief encounter, two men try to determine whether or not the girl accompanying the gold speculator is really the Daisy who was once the 'toast of the town'. In another scene, former lovers are shocked by an encounter in which each is now with another partner. Mu's use of synaesthetic imagery and repetition, a writing style that would achieve its culmination in the dreamy 'Shanghai Fox-trot', thrills the reader with the vertiginous and phantasmagoric qualities of the modern metropolis, while at the same time forcing the contemporary urban reader to look closely at him-or herself in the mirror.

This is a story that once again resonates deeply with present-day urban lifestyles in Shanghai, over eight decades after it was first penned. The superficial nature of human relationships, the shallow desire for people to seek out affirmation and adoration in the city's night-time arenas, and the need for constant escapist thrills are universal features of modern urban life, which Mu captures in this story just as sharply and colourfully as Henri de Toulouse-Lautrec did in his depictions of Montmartre cabaret culture in fin-de-siècle Paris.

Five in a Nightclub

(Translated by Randolph Trumbull)

I

Five People Beaten by Life

Saturday afternoon, 6 April 1932:

Men with blood-shot eyes milled about the gold exchange.

The price of gold came down with the speed of a twister, doing one hundred kilometres per hour. The speculators devolved into brutes. The wind blew the reason from their minds and the steel from their nerves.

Hu Junyi just laughed:

'Fools! Five more minutes and we'll be right back where we started!'

After five minutes—

'It's closing on six hundred!'

More rumours swept through the exchange: 'An earthquake has hit Japan!'

'Eighty-seven!'

'Thirty-two!'

'Zero point seventy-three!'

(A middle-aged speculator who wore poplin and sported an ivory cigarette-holder fainted dead away.)

The price of gold fell faster and faster and faster.

In five more minutes Hu Junyi was chewing his lip nervously.

When his lip shattered, a family fortune of 80,000 was swept away.

When his lip shattered, a modern businessman's heart shattered too.

Saturday afternoon, 6 April 1932:

Zheng Ping sat by the lake on campus. Lovers strolled by before his eyes. He looked this way and that. He was waiting for his darling Nina Lin.

Last night he had sent her a musical score with a few words scribbled on it: 'If you will allow me to go on living, please, meet me tomorrow at the lake on campus. My hair has turned white after what I have suffered on your account!'

Nina did not refuse the gift—and by morning Zheng Ping's hair was black once again.

After lunch he went to the appointed spot and sat there musing:

'There must be something wrong with the time. I have only waited for half an hour and yet I could swear that already I feel a five o'clock shadow on my chin.'

When Nina Lin finally came, she was with a long-legged fellow named Wang Mingxin.

'Hey, Zheng Ping,' cried Wang making a face. 'Who are you waiting for?' Zheng Ping searched Nina's face, but she just stared off into the distance. He hummed a few bars from the musical score he'd sent her:

Stranger, O stranger!
Yesterday you were my darling,
Today you say I'm a stranger.
Stranger, O stranger!
Yesterday I was your slave.
Today you say I'm a stranger.
Stranger, O stranger . . .

As Nina Lin took Wang's arm and led him away, Wang turned back to make another face. Zheng Ping bit his lip:

When his lip shattered, Zheng Ping's hair turned white.

When his lip shattered, whiskers sprouted on his chin.

Saturday afternoon, 6 April 1932:

Avenue Joffre, a boulevard transplanted from Europe.

The road down which the woman walked was soaked in golden sunlight and paved with broad shadows of leaves. A young man who was walking ahead of her turned and saw her, then spoke to his friend.

She pricked up her ears and strained to make out their conversation:

Youth A—'Isn't that Daisy Huang? She was the toast of the town five years ago!'

Youth B—'Amen. She was quite a dish!'

Youth C—'A pity we're too late! Isn't it amazing what a few years do to a woman's looks?'

A snake bit the woman's heart. She rushed across the street to look at her reflection in a shop window. One glimpse told her youth had flown from her body to lodge in that of another.

'Isn't it amazing what a few years do to a woman's looks!'

Daisy bit her lip:

When her lip shattered, her heart was swallowed by the snake.

When her lip shattered, Daisy Huang visited another French boutique.

Saturday afternoon, 6 April 1932:

Ji Jie sat in his study.

The bookcases around him were filled with different editions of *Hamlet*. Translations into Japanese, German, French, Russian, Spanish—even one done into Turkish.

Ji Jie watched the smoke from his cigarette trail upwards. It swirled and swirled.

Suddenly he felt as though the entire cosmos were a puff of smoke swirling upwards.

His Hamlets opened their mouths and began to whisper:

'What are you? What am I? What is it that you are? What is it that I am?'

Ji Jie bit his lip:

'What are you? What am I? What is it that you are? What is it that I am?'

When his lip shattered, the Hamlets laughed.

When his lip shattered, Ji Jie too dissolved into smoke and swirled upwards.

Saturday afternoon, 6 April 1932:

Town Hall.

Miao Zongdan, senior clerk, received a surprise memo from the mayor's office. In his five years at Town Hall Miao Zongdan had seen mayors come and go. He himself was like a climbing plant which grows only upwards. He had never been demoted, but he had never gotten a memo from the mayor either.

In his five years at Town Hall Miao Zongdan had copied out documents, sat on sofas, drunk tea, read newspapers; he had arrived on time and left at the proper hour. For his job Miao

Zongdan had sacrificed all the ambitions, dreams, and romantic attachments of youth.

In his five years at Town Hall Miao Zongdan had never gotten a memo from the mayor. He cut open the envelope with the same care he lavished on penning his fair copies of office documents. What? It was a letter of dismissal!

Suddenly, the end of the world.

Miao Zongdan did not believe his eyes:

'What have I done wrong?'

He read the letter again and again. Yes, there was no doubt. It was a letter of dismissal.

Miao Zongdan bit his lip:

When his lip shattered, he had no more use for the inkslab.

When his lip shattered, the head of accounting came to deliver Miao Zongdan's severance pay.

II

Saturday Night

A plate-glass revolving door: stationary it is a Dutch windmill; in motion it is a crystal pillar.

From five to six o'clock all of the thousands of automobiles of Shanghai rush westwards.

But when the doors of the office buildings are windmills, the doors of the restaurants are crystal pillars. Pedestrians stand at the kerb as street-lights wash them in a red tide and autos skim past. No sooner has the crystal pillar stopped revolving than a new crowd swims through like a school of fish.

Saturday's programme is as follows:

1. the feast (incomplete without ice-water and ice-cream);
2. pick up the woman;
3. proceed to the nightclub;
4. partake of certain refreshing amenities; ice-water, ice-cream and fruit are strictly prohibited.

(Note: You will awake Monday morning—the Sabbath being the day of rest.)

After the main course (chicken à la king) one has a bit of fruit, then a cup of café noir. The woman is as tender as the bird and as fresh as the fruit, but her soul is as black as the coffee. She is the snake that escaped from Eden!

The world of a Saturday night is a cartoon globe spinning on the axis of jazz—just as quick, just as crazed; gravity loses its pull and buildings are launched skyward.

On Saturday night reason is out of season.

On Saturday night even judges are tempted to lead lives of crime.

On Saturday night God goes to Hell.

Men out on dates completely forget the civil code against seduction. Every woman out on a date tells her man that she is not yet eighteen, all the while laughing inside over how easy he is to dupe. The driver's eyes stray from the pedestrians on the road to admire his lover's scenic contours; hands move forward to probe.

On Saturday night a self-respecting man steals; a simpleton's head fills with intrigue; a God-fearing Christian lies; old men drink rejuvenating tonics; experienced women apply kiss-proof lipstick.

Streets:

(Puyi Realty accrued annual interest totalling 33% of capital investment taels 100,000

Has Manchuria fallen

No, our volunteers are right now fighting in the snow
with Japs to the last man

COUNTRYMEN COME PLEDGE MONTHLY
DONATIONS

The Mainland Daily circulation now totals 50,000

1933 Bartok

free meal-line)

'Evening Post!' The newsboy opened his blue mouth to reveal blue teeth and a blue tongue. The blue neon high-heeled shoe across from him pointed straight at his mouth.

'Evening Post!' Suddenly the boy's mouth turned red. He stuck out a red tongue to catch wine being poured from an enormous neon bottle across the street.

Red streets, green streets, blue streets, purple streets . . . City clad in strong colours! Dancing neon light—multi-coloured waves, scintillating waves, colourless waves—a sky filled with colour. The sky now had everything: wine, cigarettes,high-heels, clock-towers . . .

Try White Horse whisky! Chesterfield cigarettes are kind to the smoker's throat.

Alexander's Shoestore, Johnson's Bar, Laslo's Tobacco Shop, Dizzy's Music World, chocolate and candy shops, the Empire Cinema, Hamilton Travel Agency . . .

Swirling, endlessly swirling neon lights—

Suddenly the neon lights focus:

EMPRESS NIGHTCLUB

When the doors are open the face of the Sikh doorman appears; now he is gone, the door is closed. Before the door there

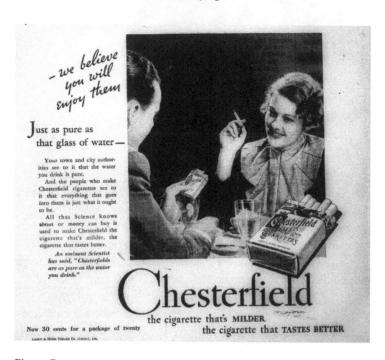

Figure 7
Chesterfield cigarettes advertisement, *North-China Daily News*, 10 May
1934.

stands a man in blue with his arms full of white Pekinese dogs. *Yap, yap, yap.*

A bullfrog flounders forwards. Bulging eyes staring, belly tight to the ground, the frog gives out a croak and stops before the glass door. Then an automobile pulls up and a woman gets out, her head bent low. She is followed by a gentleman in tails who steps up to offer his arm.

'Oh, let's buy a puppy.'

The man produces a bill then hands his date a dog.

'What do I get in return?'

The woman sticks out her tongue and wrinkles her nose.

'Charming, Dear!' he says.

She squeezes the dog and runs into the nightclub as the pet yammers in protest.

III

Five Happy People

Tablecloths: white linen, white linen, white linen—white . . .

On the white linen: dark beer and black coffee—darkness, blackness . . .

By the white tablecloths sit men dressed in formal evening attire: layers of black and white: black hair, white faces, black eyes, white collars, black ties, white starched shirts, black jackets, white waistcoats, black pants . . . black and white . . .

Beyond the tablecloths stand the waiters in their white suits and black caps. Black piping runs down their white pants . . .

White man's happiness, black man's misery. Music from the cannibal rituals of Africa; the loud-soft thunder of drums, the trumpet's wail, and in the centre of the dance floor a row of indigent Russian princesses performing the black man's tap-dance; scores of white legs kick below black-clad torsoes:

Duh-duh-duh-duh-da!

More layers of black and white! Why is it that two white patches are sewn into the black silk wrapping their breasts, and why is there a third white patch over the belly? Tap-dancing, Russian princesses; dancing, the white legs, the white chests and belly; dancing, the layers of white and black . . . the layers of white and black.

Everyone contracts this malaria. Fevered music; ah, the deadly mosquitoes of African jungles.

The white puppy barks outside on the stairs. The plate-glass door swings open and in walks the lady followed by the gentleman.

The woman cried out in delight. 'Pigiloff's hunting-dance!'

'Yes, quite a sight!'

A conversation among the clientele:

'Look, it's Hu Junyi! Hu Junyi is here.'

'The middle-aged man standing over at the door?'

'Yes.'

'Who did he bring?'

'Daisy Huang, of course! What's the matter with you? You don't even know Daisy Huang?'

'That can't be her! I know Daisy Huang when I see her.'

'She's Daisy Huang, I tell you. I'm willing to put money on it.'

'But this woman is too young! She couldn't be Daisy Huang!'

'What do you mean, 'too young'? Daisy Huang is only in her thirties, you know.'

'Is that woman in her thirties? She's not even twenty.'

'It is pointless to argue. I say she's Daisy Huang and you don't believe me, right? Fine, whoever is wrong buys the next bottle. Go take a closer look.'

On Daisy Huang's laughing face, below her Norma Shearer hairdo, only one eye was visible, the wrinkles around it cleverly concealed by make-up. The shadow under her nose obscured lines at the corners of her mouth. But even laughter could not hide the weariness in her eye. A trumpet blared. The two-tone Russian princesses moved off the dance floor and across to the white table-cloths, melting one by one into the crowd of dark-suited men. A cymbal crashed like a glass plate hitting the floor. The last princess on the dance floor suddenly shortened by half, then disappeared completely.

The applause nearly blasted the building to pieces.

Daisy Huang tossed her dog into the lap of Hu Junyi in order to free her hands for clapping. Hu Junyi's hands, already engaged in clapping, fumbled for a moment in order to catch the animal. Hu laughed.

Back to the customers' dialogue:

'Very well, I'll accept the wager. I'm sure that woman isn't Daisy Huang—no, wait just a moment: what I mean is that Daisy Huang isn't that young. Daisy Huang's almost thirty. Since you insist that she is Daisy Huang, you've got to ask her age. If she says she's younger than twenty-five we'll know first that she is not Daisy Huang and second that you'll buy the drinks.'

'What if she's older?'

'Then I'll buy.'

'Fair enough. You won't welsh, will you?'

'Just shut up and get over there.'

Daisy Huang and Hu Junyi sat close to the white cloth covering their table. A waiter was pouring an orange liquor into tall-stemmed glasses from a bottle he had swathed in a white napkin. As he watched their glasses fill Hu Junyi murmured:

'Your lips are as red as wine, but the wine of your lips is far more sweet.'

'Silly!'

'Just a few words from a song.'

Daisy laughed.

'Excuse me, I would like to know whether you are in your twenties or your thirties.'

Daisy Huang wheeled around and saw Customer A standing at her shoulder. She just gaped at the man, wondering to whom he could possibly have addressed such a question.

'Perhaps you didn't hear me. I asked whether you are twenty years of age, or thirty years of age. You see, my friends and I have a—'

'I beg your pardon?'

'What I mean to ask is, are you somewhere in the vicinity of twenty years old? Or can it be that you are nearer—'

Daisy Huang felt the snake biting her heart once more. She shot up out of her chair and slapped the man in the face, hard, then fell back into her chair and began to cry.

Hu Junyi rose: 'What did you mean by that remark, sir?'

Customer A stood there rubbing his cheek: 'I . . . I'm sorry. Please excuse me, I mistook the lady for someone else.' He gave a slight bow then lurched off.

'Don't take it so hard, Daisy. You heard the idiot: he thought you were somebody else.'

'Do I really look all that old, Junyi?'

'What? Old? Of course not! You'll always be young to me!'

This got her laughing. 'Oh, I'll always be young to "you", eh? Ha, I'll always be young!' She lifted her glass. 'A toast! A toast to the eternal youth of Daisy Huang!'

Daisy drained her glass and then slumped over against Hu, weak with laughter.

'Daisy, what's the matter? Don't make such a fuss! What's the matter with you? You're acting crazy!' he said, squeezing the dog. The dog began to whine.

'I've never been more sane in my life!' said Daisy, who had regained her composure. Suddenly she laughed again: 'I will always be young. Oh, Junyi, let's make a real night of it!' Daisy pulled Hu Junyi out onto the dance floor.

A vacated table.

The couples at nearby tables whispered.

'That woman is mad!'

'She is Daisy Huang, isn't she?'

'Mm. She's getting on, after all.'

'And that man with her, he looks like Hu Junyi. I met him once at a dinner party.'

'You're right, that is Hu Junyi, the gold baron.'

'But the other day I heard that he lost his entire fortune on the gold exchange.'

'Yes, I've also heard rumours to that effect. But just today I saw him driving around in the same old Lincoln, taking Daisy Huang to all the shops, buying her expensive things . . . He has been in gold for quite a while. I find it hard to believe that a man of his experience could lose every last penny on the exchange.'

The glass door swung open again, this time to admit a burst of raucous laughter and a man in his twenties supported by another man of the same age. By their side, slightly to the rear, was a rather young, very nervous woman. When the first youth through the door caught sight of the nightclub manager's bald head, he reached up and drew a line across it with his thumb:

'Slick as a whistle!'

Whereupon he buckled over and staggered backwards in hysterics.

Everyone turned to look:

A tuxedo stained by wine, a lock of hair hanging across his forehead; eyes, watery and feverish; cheeks a blotchy red. A handkerchief dangling precariously from his breast pocket.

'Why, the blighter is drunk.'

'Just look at him!'

The manager whose bald head had just been drawn on ran over to help support the youth, then inquired of his companion where he had been drinking.

'At a hotel! Imagine, he gets this tight and still insists on coming here.' The friend lowered his voice: 'Do you know whether Miss Lin is here? Nina Lin?'

'Yes, as a matter of fact, I believe she is!'

'Who's she with?'

A young woman at a table nearby turned to her escort: 'Let's go. That sot just came in!'

'You aren't scared of Zheng Ping, are you?'

'Of course not. It's just that he's drunk and I don't want him to make a scene in public.'

'We can't leave without passing by in front of him.'

'I don't care,' the woman said dreamily. 'I just want to go . . . '

The man leaned forward: 'Anything you say, Nina, my sweet!'

Nina rose and started for the door with her date close behind.

The manager motioned with his head. 'Isn't that Miss Lin right there?'

'He's right,' cried the young woman who had arrived with Zheng Ping and his friend. 'Isn't that Leggy Wang?'

'Oh for heaven's sake, here comes the showdown.'

Wang Mingxin and Nina Lin walked directly towards them, but when Nina Lin neared Zheng Ping she had a sudden loss of nerve. She called out softly: 'Mingxin.'

'Don't be frightened, Nina, I'm right behind you!'

Zheng Ping was still laughing—laughing so hard that tears were streaming down his face—but when he caught sight of Nina walking towards him, he cried out ecstatically.

'Nina!'

Then he wiped the tears from his face and got a clearer view. There, arm in arm with Nina Lin, was Wang Mingxin.

'Nina . . . Oh, you, huh? Why don't you just go to hell!'

Zheng Ping struggled to free his arm but his friend clamped it tight and guided him forward into the club. 'You were mistaken. That was a different couple.' The young lady who had come in with Zheng paused for a curt nod to Nina. Nina smiled distantly, then lowered her head and walked out the door with Wang Mingxin, who glared at Zheng Ping. A new couple came in just as they passed through, so that as the neon light from the club's sign flashed across the glass door—

A thought suddenly flashed through Wang's mind: 'Are my eyes deceiving me or is that Zhijun? Zhijun, the girl who dumped me! How come she's going out with Miao Zongdan?'

A thought suddenly dashed through Zhijun's mind: 'So Wang Mingxin has yet another new girlfriend!'

Wang pushed open the door on the left. Zhijun came through the door on the right. The plate-glass moved, a red glimmer from the neon light flashed across its surface, and Wang wrapped his arm around Nina's shoulder, saying: 'Dear!'

Zhijun straightaway put her arm through Miao Zongdan's and raised her head slightly: 'Zongdan . . .' In Miao Zongdan's head swirled these words: 'This note informs Mr. Miao Zongdan, from the mayor's own pen, from the mayor's own pen, this note informs Mr. Miao Zongdan . . .'

The door closed and its green drapery separated Wang and his date from Miao Zongdan and his. In the vestibule Miao Zongdan spied a band-member, drummer 'Johnny' Johnson, who seemed to be headed past him for the exit. Miao waved.

'Hullo, Johnny!'

Johnson's eyes darted across to Miao's face, but he went right by and out the door, yelling over his shoulder: 'Can't talk now. Be right back.'

No sooner had Miao Zongdan found a table and seated Zhijun than he saw a tousle-headed man seated across from them gesture vehemently; in so doing, he upset a wine-glass and the orange-coloured liquor spattered Hu Junyi's pants. Hu was deep in conversation with Daisy Huang, but Daisy, who saw the whole thing coming, jumped up in fright.

Hu Junyi clambered to his feet: 'How did that happen?'

Daisy Huang stared at Zheng Ping, but he just cocked his head and glared right back. 'Oh, why don't you go to hell too!'

Zheng's friend pushed him back down into his chair and made a hasty explanation: 'I'm terribly sorry! As you see, my friend has had a bit too much to drink.'

'That's all right.' As Hu Junyi took out his handkerchief and turned to assist Daisy, he noticed that it was his own pants that were soiled. He couldn't help laughing.

A number of waiters rushed over, whereupon Miao's view of the scene was obscured.

Johnson came back into the club and sat down by Zhijun.

'How is it going, baby?'

'Fine, thanks.'

'Johnny, you look very sad!'

Johnson shrugged, then laughed.

'What's wrong?'

'My wife has gone into labour. Just now she called and asked me to come home. You saw me run out to answer the phone, right? But the manager won't give me permission.' Before he could explain further, a waiter dashed over. 'Mr. Johnson, there's another call for you.' Again Johnson ran out.

By the time the lights came back up, Hu Junyi's table was again set up with glasses of orange-coloured liquor. Hu's face was bent close to that of Daisy Huang. Zheng Ping, his hair turned white from worry, sat quietly as his friends wiped the sweat from their faces with handkerchiefs. Zhijun felt someone's eyes on the back of her neck. When she turned around to look, she saw it was Ji Jie. His eyes were dark as night. She couldn't tell how deep they were, or what it was that they held.

'Won't you join us?'

'No, I'll stay here by myself.'

'Why are you sitting off in a corner?'

'I like it. It's quiet.'

'Did you come here alone?'

'Yes. I like solitude.'

His zombie gaze fell slowly until it came to rest on the black heels of her shoes.

She shuddered and turned back to Miao Zongdan.

'Who's that?'

'Somebody from school. He graduated when I was a freshman.'

Miao Zongdan was breaking matchsticks in half and lining up the pieces in the ash-tray.

'Are you feeling OK, Zongdan?'

'Hm?' He looked up at her, then stretched. 'Yes, of course.'

'You can settle down. You know, get married.'

'I haven't got the money.'

'How can it be that a government salary isn't enough? And here you are, such an able man!'

'Able—' Miao Zongdan began, then quickly broke off, deciding not to tell her about the note. At this juncture Johnson returned from outside and approached their table.

'Well? What news?'

Johnson stopped in front of them and spoke rather slowly. 'It was a baby boy, but he died. They say my wife fainted. They're telling me to come home, but I can't.'

'Why did she faint?'

'I don't know.' Johnson remained silent a while. 'At the moment I most want to cry they tell me to laugh.'

'I'm sorry for you, Johnny!'

'Let's cheer up!' Johnson emptied a tumbler of whisky in a single gulp, stood up, and suddenly began to leap around slapping his knees. 'Here, look at me! I have wings! I can fly, fly, fly!' Johnson capered around the nightclub.

Zhijun bent over laughing, Daisy Huang covered her mouth with a handkerchief, Miao Zongdan roared, Zheng Ping doubled up with laughter. Hu Junyi quickly swallowed a mouthful of drink in order to join in the mirth.

Ha, ha, ha! Ha! Ha! Ha, ha, ha!

Daisy Huang had thrown her handkerchief off somewhere. She leaned back against the chair and tilted her head to laugh facing the red neon lights directly above. Everyone laughed with her—open mouths, open mouths, open mouths . . . gaping holes that with every passing moment seemed less human. Everyone's face changed: Zheng Ping had a sharp chin, Hu Junyi a round one. Miao Zongdan's chin had somehow left his face completely, as if it had grown directly from the Adam's apple. Wrinkles filled the area under Daisy's chin.

The only person not laughing was Ji Jie, who quietly watched with eyes as sharp as scalpels, ears pricked up like a hunting dog in a forest waiting to devour each laugh.

When Miao Zongdan noticed Ji Jie's scalpel gaze, he suddenly heard his laughter as it was, and the laughter of the others too: 'What a weird noise!'

Hu Junyi also noticed Ji Jie: 'Can it possibly be me who's laughing?'

Daisy Huang foggily remembered when as a child she awoke from a nightmare and felt for the first time the terror of a dark room: 'I'm scared!'

Zheng Ping, groggily: 'Are these voices human? How can these people be laughing?'

All four of them fell silent. Around the club a few more of the revellers were still struggling to control themselves, but very soon they too stopped laughing. They were in the clutches of a strange blend of fear and loneliness: the feeling experienced by a man in the woods late at night who is suddenly deprived of the warmth of fire and friend.

Then a cymbal crashed and Johnson was with the band on the stage.

'Cheer up, ladies and gentlemen!'

Johnson's drums created a syncopated hurricane. Couples were swept out onto the dancefloor. Daisy Huang dragged Hu Junyi out; Miao Zongdan tossed the mayor's letter away; even Zheng Ping stood up, only to find that his friend's arm had encircled the young lady's waist.

'They got away, all of them!' Zheng Ping covered his face with his hands and sat there reckoning that for him there was no question of escape. Suddenly he felt clear in the head, just as though he had never gotten drunk at all. He looked up and saw the couple whose drinks he had spilled; their steps were so quick that they seemed frenzied. A couple whirled by and disappeared, then another. 'I'll never get away, never!' No sooner had he resolved to try to escape than he caught Ji Jie staring across the room at him.

Zheng Ping got up and walked over to join Ji at his table: 'My friend, let me tell you a joke.' Zheng Ping droned on like a gramophone. Ji Jie watched him in silence, thinking: 'What are you? What am I? What is it that I am? What is it that you are?'

The eyes that stared back at Zheng Ping might have been made of stone for all the life they had. Zheng Ping just ignored the man's gaze and went on talking and laughing.

Zhijun and Miao Zongdan returned from the dance floor and sat on a table. Zhijun was slightly out of breath. She began listening to Zheng Ping's jokes, but no sooner did she begin to laugh softly than Miao Zongdan led her back for another dance. Ji Jie listened to Zheng Ping as his hands busied themselves snapping matchsticks. When the matchsticks were gone he tore up the matchboxes, and when those were gone he asked the waiter for more.

The waiter returned with a fresh box: 'Sir, your table is littered with matchsticks!'

'Yes. You see, in four seconds a single matchstick can be broken into eight sections, therefore we proceed at a rate of one and a half boxes per hour. Right now it is . . . Excuse me, you have the correct time, don't you?'

'Yes, sir. It's almost two.'

'Very well, I shall leave in six boxes.' Ji Jie returned to snapping matches.

The waiter rolled his eyes and departed.

The customers' conversation:

Customer C: 'He is a character, isn't he, coming to a night-club to break matchsticks. Why doesn't he just buy a dollar's worth of them at the store? That would have kept him busy snapping at home the whole day long.'

Customer D: 'He who has nothing to do after dinner and who can come here to break matchsticks is a happy man.'

Customer C: 'Even the drunkard with him is happy! He's the guy who spilled the drink after barging in here. A while ago he was picking fights, now he's telling jokes!'

Customer D: 'Everyone over on this side is happy. Look over there at Daisy Huang and Hu Junyi, and the couple next to them. Now that is dancing!'

Customer C: 'You bet! They'll dance till they drop. By the way, what time is it?'

Customer D: 'After two.'

Customer C: 'Shall we go? Most everyone has.'

The plate-glass door opened, allowing a couple to run out. The man's tie was loose and the woman's hair was mussed.

The plate-glass door opened again, allowing another couple to escape. The man's tie was loose and the woman's hair was mussed.

The dance hall quieted down as it emptied. The manager paced back and forth, his shining pate alternately red, green, blue, and white.

Hu Junyi sat down and pulled out a handkerchief to wipe the perspiration from his neck: 'Let's sit this one out, shall we?'

Daisy replied: 'If you want to. But why shouldn't we keep on dancing? Today is my twenty-eighth birthday, and tomorrow I'll be a day older. Every day is precious to a woman; every day makes a difference. Let's dance while I'm young! Why shouldn't we dance?'

'Daisy—' Hu Junyi, handkerchief still in hand, was again dragged to the dance floor.

As Miao Zongdan danced he noticed a sagging string of helium balloons above his head. He jumped up and snatched one down, then he patted Zhijun on the cheek with it and instructed her: 'Hold on to this! This is the world!' Zhijun took the balloon and held it between their faces, laughing:

'Then you're in the western hemisphere and I'm in the eastern one!'

Someone must have pricked their balloon, because it popped. Miao Zongdan's smiling face suddenly grew serious: 'That was the world! That balloon which popped . . . that popped balloon!' Miao Zongdan pushed his chest against Zhijun's and skated through the crowd, weaving in search of dancing room.

'Enough, enough,' laughed Zhijun as she gasped for breath. 'Zongdan, one more step and I'll collapse.'

'You're still fine! Come on, it's past three o'clock now and the club closes at four. Not much longer to go. Dance! Come on, keep dancing!' They jostled the next couple.

'Sorry!' and off they sped again.

Ji Jie by now had covered the floor with broken matchsticks. One box, two boxes, three boxes, four boxes, five boxes . . .

Zheng Ping was still sitting there with him, laughing, telling jokes, not really caring what he said.

Their waiter yawned.

Zheng Ping abruptly fell silent.

'Need to wet that whistle of yours?' chuckled Ji Jie, slipping out of character.

Zheng Ping hummed:

> *Stranger, O stranger!*
> *Yesterday you were my darling,*
> *Today you say I'm a stranger.*
> *Stranger, O stranger!*

Ji Jie glanced at his watch. He put down the matchbox and rubbed his hands:

'Twenty minutes to go.'

Time's footsteps beat a soft but steady tread into the heart of Zheng Ping. Seconds crawled like ants over his heart—one after another—quickly and endlessly, marching on and on and on—'Oh, the tilt of Nina's head as she lifts her lips to Wang's! After a second she will tilt further, and after another second further still, then further and further and further until who knows what posture she has ended up in by now.' Zheng Ping felt his heart shrink. 'Tell more jokes!' But he could remember none.

Time's footsteps beat a soft but steady tread into the heart of Daisy Huang. Seconds crawled like ants over her heart— one after another— quickly and endlessly, marching on and on and on—'I'm growing older with every second! "Amazing what five years does to a woman's looks." Perhaps tomorrow morning I'll see an old hag in the mirror.'

Daisy Huang felt her heart shrink. 'Dance faster!' But there was no strength in her legs. Time's footsteps beat a soft but steady tread into the heart of Hu Junyi. Seconds crawled like ants over his heart—one after another—quickly and endlessly, marching on and on and on—'Tomorrow morning the gold baron Hu Junyi will be ruined! The courts, the auctioneers, jail . . .' Hu Junyi felt his heart shrink. He remembered the bottle of sleeping pills on his night-table, the steak knife in the dining room, the pistol of his blue-blooded Russian bodyguard out in the parking lot, its six-inch barrel and black muzzle . . . 'What lies inside this mysterious little hole?' Hu Junyi suddenly wanted to sleep. He longed for the black muzzle.

Time's footsteps beat a soft but steady tread into the heart of Miao Zongdan. Seconds crawled like ants over his heart—one after another—quickly and endlessly, marching on and on and on—'On Monday I will be a free man. No more documents to copy, no more racing at dawn to Fenglin Bridge, no more windy bus rides to work on route 22. Yes, I will be a free man.' Miao Zongdan felt his heart shrink. 'Take your pleasure while you can! Drink up! No salary from tomorrow!' Who at Town Hall would believe that such reckless thoughts could fill the head of a man like Miao Zongdan? Inconceivable. But on some days anything is possible.

One by one the young women sitting by the white tablecloths prepared to leave.

They opened their purses, took out compacts, powdered their noses in the tiny mirrors.

'What wouldn't a man do for a beauty like me—' But they only saw a nose, or an eye, or the curve of a lip, or a wisp of hair; they didn't see the whole face. The men lit up their last cigarettes.

'Good night, my darling!' The quick, sassy sound of the next tune floated across from the bandstand.

'The last song!' yelled everyone, crowding out to dance. The club: rows and rows of soiled tablecloths, bored waiters lounging in dark corners with brooms in hand, the glowing head of the manager moving hither and thither. The glass door was open for a continuous stream of departing customers who moved from a dream into bright corridors beyond. With a single thump the bass drum brought the lights of the establishment up to full strength. The musicians bent over and put away their instruments, the waiters emerged with their brooms, the manager stood in the doorway wishing his customers good night. In no time the club was empty. All that was left was an empty room, untidy and silent, and an empty dance floor. The bright lights had dissolved the dreams. Miao Zongdan stood by his table, a popped balloon.

Daisy Huang cast a look at him, a popped balloon.

Hu Junyi sighed, a popped balloon.

Zheng Ping, a popped balloon, felt his flushed cheeks.

Ji Jie, a popped balloon, regarded the chandelier hanging in the centre of the room.

What was a balloon? And what was a popped balloon?

Johnson walked frowning back into the club.

'Goodnight, Johnny!' cried Miao Zongdan.

'My wife died too!'

'I'm awfully sorry for you Johnny!' Miao Zongdan patted him on the back.

'Are you leaving?'

'I don't know. I suppose it's all the same whether we leave or not.'

Daisy Huang—'Wherever I go, I'll never retrieve my youth!'

Zheng Ping—'Wherever I go, Nina will not come back to me!'

Hu Junyi—'Wherever I go, I'll never get my fortune back.'

'Hold on! Let me play one more song for everyone to dance to, all right?'

'Sure, Johnny.'

Johnson walked over to the orchestra pit, picked up a violin and carried it to the centre of the dance floor. He cradled the instrument under his chin, set the bow to its strings and played a slow, sad tune. Tears ran from his brown eyes down his cheeks and onto the violin strings. The three tired couples, parted from their souls, slowly danced in a ring around the musician. *Ping!* A string on Johnson's violin broke. His arms fell limp to his sides.

I can't help it!'

The couples stopped dancing to stare at him.

Zheng Ping shrugged: 'No one can help it!'

Ji Jie looked at the useless violin and blurted: '*C'est toute sa vie!*'

A soft voice breathed in the ears of all five of them: 'No one can help it!'

Not a word was uttered. They slowly dragged themselves out the door— bodies tired, minds spent.

Outside near the car of Hu Junyi there was a loud bang. Was it a blow-out or a pistol shot?

Hu Junyi, the gold baron, lay on the sidewalk with a bullet-wound in his temple, his bloody face contorted in the agony of death. Daisy Huang sat stunned in his car. A crowd of people gathered. They asked in loud voices what had happened. They jostled, debated, lamented, and dispersed. The sky slowly grew light. Outside the Empress Nightclub a few people ringed the corpse of Hu Junyi. Johnson, Ji Jie, Miao Zongdan, Daisy Huang and Zheng Ping stood in silent contemplation.

IV

Four at a Funeral

On 10 April 1932, four people left the International Cemetery after witnessing the interment of Hu Junyi. The group was comprised of white-haired Zheng Ping, unemployed Miao Zongdan, Daisy Huang (now four days past her twenty-eighth birthday) and Ji Jie, whose eyes cut like scalpels.

Daisy Huang—'How tired I am of life!'

Miao Zongdan—'At least Hu Junyi is beyond life's torment. It would be sweet to enjoy such a rest!'

Zheng Ping—'I have an old man's heart!'

Ji Jie—'Nothing of what any one of you says makes the least sense to me.'

They all fell silent.

A freight train chugged by. Rolling, rolling, rolling down tracks that stretched out of sight, it let out a sigh.

Sprawling city, unending journey!

They stared sadly at one another for a moment, then started back—walking, walking, walking. Before them lay a long and lonesome road . . .

Sprawling city, unending journey!

3

Craven 'A'

(1932)

'Craven "A"' is the name of a popular cigarette brand from the 1930s. It is also the nickname that the narrator of this story gives to a dance hall girl, whose name is Yu Huixian. The story focuses on the brief romantic affair between the male narrator—a lawyer and an upstanding member of the Shanghai bourgeoisie—and this mysterious twenty-year-old dance hostess. In a passage famous among scholars of modern Chinese fiction, the narrator begins the story by describing a journey taken by the eyes along the physical plane of her body, imagining it to be the geographic landscape of a country. He then enters into a brief relationship with the girl, despite the warnings of his friends. Even in the sensuous world of dance halls in Shanghai, Craven 'A' has a reputation as a vixen, and the other hostesses regard her with apathy and disdain.

Early on in the story, it is made clear that she has many male friends, though the sexual dimensions of her relations with men, and with the narrator, are left somewhat ambiguous. The only unambiguous sexual encounter is the one that she relates to the narrator, describing how an amorous pursuer took her virginity at the age of seventeen. Since then, Craven 'A' has been on a downward spiral, loving men and being loved by them, but only briefly and furtively. Mu uses the English word 'cheap' repeatedly to describe the hostess, although the narrator shows a great deal of sympathy for her situation. Even so, it is left ambiguous as to whether she is being played around with by men, or if she herself is the player.

This is one of the most psychologically rich depictions of a young girl caught up in the world of Chinese dance halls during the jazz age. In addition to his virtuosic rendition of her body through the metaphor of geography, Mu layers the story with thick and dreamy descriptions of the city landscape at night, evoking a picturesque landscape that might have been painted by Parisian surrealist artists of the same era. The narrator himself remains distant and analytical, in the fashion of a lawyer, showing sympathy for the girl but also refusing to fall too deeply into the trap of her young love.

For Mu, the lesson about getting one's fingers burned had been learned after the experience of 'The Man Who Was Treated as a Plaything', and his stories about dance hall hostesses and their bodies take on the coldly analytical style of a medical doctor. His reference to the girl as a mannequin as he undresses her in one scene reminds the scholar of a later story that Mu wrote, 'Statue of a Platinum Nude', featuring a doctor undressing a lovely young woman. The story 'Craven "A"' provides a feast for the imagination, casting a burning light onto the cold and cruel world of fast, commercialized romance in the dance halls of the modern metropolis.

Craven 'A'

The particular scent of Craven 'A' wafted over slowly from amid the jazz. I turned my head around—eeh, it was her again! Sitting over there at a table, quietly smoking a cigarette. I'd bumped into her quite often, a small squarish Parisian face, and a girl who brought a different guy every time. From the first time I saw her, I paid special attention to her. Her eyes had two different expressions: when she was smoking Craven 'A' brand cigarettes, her eyes were like a light-grey Viyella fabric—from inside the thin haze of cigarette smoke, her gaze was so unfocused, as if she couldn't see anybody, and without any purpose or intent was looking straight ahead. When she was using the mirror from her purse to powder her nose, when she was dancing, when she was laughing, when she was talking, she had a sly, rat-like pair of deep black eyes, from the edge of the mirror, from the shoulder of her dance partner, from above the glass of alcohol, she glanced nimbly at people, as if she intended to capture away every man's soul.

Carefully studying her—this was one of my hobbies. A person's face is a map. When one has studied the terrain, the mountains, rivers, climate, rainfall, the folk customs of the region, one can

Figure 8
Craven 'A' cigarettes advertisement, *North-China Daily News*, 10 May 1934.

Figures 9–12

Viyella advertisements, *Zhongyang ribao*, 5 May 1929.

immediately grasp the characteristics of the person. In front of me was an excellent national map:

On the northern borderlands was a black pine forest zone. The demarcation of the border zone was a white silk headband, like a band of white clouds in a sky blanketed by coal smoke. The black pine forest zone was a manufacturing place for spices. Heading south was a large flat plain, a white marble plain, a place of origin for a resourceful and clever nation. Under that was a verdant peak, and on the east and west of the peak were two long and narrow zones of fibrous grasslands. According to legend, in ancient times this was a nest for witches. Next to the grasslands were two lakes. The people who lived there had dual ethnic characteristics: the pessimism typical of northerners, and the affability of southerners. The climate was variable: sometimes it dipped under the freezing point, and sometimes it reached above the boiling point; there was a violent seasonal wind, but the rainfall was very low. This point on the high peak was a volcano—the mouth of the volcano opened slightly and out poured Craven 'A' smoke. From inside the volcanic crater, one could see orderly, milk-white lava rocks—amid the lava rocks moved a flame. This volcano was a sign that under the earth was hidden a storehouse of passion. The people of this region were very primitive. Every year they sacrificed men to the volcano. For travellers, this country was not at all a safe place. After the volcano there was a sea cliff.

The map below was covered by a black-and-white chessboard pattern; below that, plain and sparse cloud! But one could still discern the lay of the land. Passing by the sea cliff, one had already reached the interior. There was an expanse of fertile flatlands. By the ups and downs and elasticity of the land on the horizon, one could conjecture that this area had a very deep layer of clay. The climate was temperate, and the average temperature was seventy-five degrees; the rainfall was neither great nor little; the earth was moist. A twin pair of small mountains stubbornly confronted each other on the plain, their purple peaks projecting faintly out of the clouds. This must have been a famous scenic spot. Playfully thinking about the writings and poems on the stone tablet upon the peaks, at the same time I was arranging a plan to visit in the future. But the national defence of this country was weak, there was no fortification above the sea cliff, so if one launched a surprise attack from here, within an hour one could occupy the fertile plain and the scenic region. Looking southward from there, one only saw that the fertile plain turned into a declivity, which receded evenly downward—the map below was blocked by the table situated horizontally at the centre!

The south had a spring breeze that was even more intoxicating than the north, even more fertile land, even more enchanting lakes, even more mysterious mountains and valleys, even more beautiful scenery!

Longing, I lowered my head. Below the table were two sea walls. Looking through the fishnet stockings, I saw mud in the colour of milky-white mandarin fish.[1] At the far end of the sea walls slept two slim, black-mouthed white gulls, silently dreaming early summer dreams, at the edge of that quiet and secluded shore. Between the two sea walls, inferring from the topography, there should be a triangular alluvial plain, and the place that met the sea must be an important harbour, a large port of trade. Otherwise, why would they have built such an exquisite pair of sea walls? The nightscape of the metropolis was lovely—think about the colours of the setting sun on the sea wall, the sound of waves at the docks, the majestic posture of the large ocean vessels entering the port, the spray of waves at the bow of the ships, the tall constructions pressing against the shoreline.

The two gulls had awakened, and were flying over the ocean in the clear sky to the tune of 'Goodnight, Vienna', freely and easily, playing amid some fur seals, some yellow sharks, and some black whales. Craven 'A' was burning lonesomely on the table.

'That girl, the one that I bump into often, sitting at that table there with the small square face, wearing an outfit of black and white checks, do you know her?' I asked Haowen, when he was about to stand up.

'That one, you say?' He sat down again.

'Yes, that one, dancing with a man with a little moustache.'

At that moment she and Little Moustache danced by the front of our table, she saw Haowen, and nodded her head.

'That's her!'

'Her? That's the Hot Baby that I told you about last time!' Haowen began to laugh, and looked at his dance partner, Miss Lin Taili.

Miss Lin pursed her lips and said, 'Why are you staring at me?'

Haowen said to me, 'Well? Do you want to meet her?'

I said, 'I've thought about it for a long time. She's an interesting character.'

'Stop talking about it. If you keep talking about this, our Miss Lin will become unhappy.'

'Why? Does Miss Lin not get along with her?'

'It's not that I don't get along with her, I don't even know her, it's only—but, why do you men all love getting to know her? Such a small square face, I really don't see what's so pretty about her?'

Haowen whispered in my ear, 'The lady you mentioned is Yu Huixian, the one and only Yu Huixian.'

'That's her?'

I knew many of her stories—almost all of my friends had travelled in this country before, because the transportation was convenient. Within around one or two days one could travel around the entire country. On the tops of those twin peaks, they had all written their lines of poetry. As for the more experienced ones, as soon as they arrived they climbed to shore from the harbour, and then turned against the current and headed northward. Some lingered for a day or two, others hung around for a week. Upon their return they boasted to me about the majestic beauty of the scenery of this land. Everyone took this place as an excellent spot for a short-term visit.

Haowen continued with his story: 'You know, we've all told her we loved her, but who really loves her? So cheap! Sure she's a real fine gal, and you can play with her all right, but if you really fell in love with her, it'd be a disaster! In Hong Kong, one man even died for her, and one man was sent to prison. Look at her having fun here, what a dangerous woman. If you want me to introduce you . . . '

I nodded my head.

(A woman taken lightly by others a majestic scenic spot temporarily visited at the dance hall ocean water bathhouse movie theatre suburbs garden park growing in Hong Kong played around with playing with others taken lightly taken lightly pushed aside by society unfortunate person)

Suddenly, I experienced a kind of sympathy for her, a sort of pity: 'Does she herself know that she's been taken lightly and played around with by others?'—so was I thinking.

A song ended, and as she walked in front of our table and returned to her own table, she was grabbed by Haowen.

'Sit here for a spell.'

She sat down, and looking at me said, 'Haowen, are you introducing me to another new friend?'

'That's right, Mr. Yuan Yecun, this is Miss Yu Huixian.'

'Mr. Yuan, please come to my table and bring some cigarettes.'

'I have some already.'

'No. I want Craven "A".'

'Why do you want Craven "A"?'

'I love the faint, light-grey taste.'

So I went over to her table, and brought over the red matchbox with the black cat crouching on the cover, struck a match for her, and lit it: 'I'll call you Miss Craven "A".'

'Careful, black cats are evil omens.'

'Black cats also symbolize good fortune.'

Suddenly she said, 'Sit over here a bit, I want to say something to you.' She gestured at me with her hand as if she was going to tell me a secret. I leaned my head over. She whispered to me, 'I will call you Black Cat, okay?'—So innocently. I laughed.

Miss Lin gave a cold laugh in her nose. Her gaze was telling me, 'Isn't it so? So cheap!' I felt bad for Craven 'A'. I looked at her, and she happily laughed, seemingly not understanding Miss Lin's smile.

She only took two puffs, and then handed me her cigarette stained with lipstick. While puffing on this honey-tasting cigarette, I asked her, 'How come you aren't smoking it, after I took such great pains to get it for you?'

'Only when I have nothing to do, or when I'm bored, do I smoke.'

'You aren't bored now are you?'

She nodded her head.

'Why aren't you bored?'

'Because—come here!'

I leaned my ear over. She looked at Haowen, and whispered into my ear, 'Because you have a cute-looking face!' Saying this, she covered her mouth and laughed. Suddenly I felt somebody give my leg a little kick, and when I looked down, I only saw the two black-mouthed gulls flying back, and hiding under her chair. When I lifted my head again, she was stealing a look at me from between her fingers. Confronted with her irrepressible temerity, I could only respond like a fool: 'Naughty child!' Suddenly she covered my mouth with her hand and told me to stop talking, and she took the cigarette back out of my hand, sat there quietly, emitting light-grey puffs of smoke. Her face wasn't smiling, and she didn't have that crafty, rat-like look in her eyes. What did I see? I saw a pair of light-grey, Viyella fabric-coloured eyes.

Floating over from the music stage was a sentimental, tired melody called 'The Last Rose of Summer', a folk tune that I knew very well.

> 'Tis the last rose of summer
> Left blooming alone.

She sat quietly. I sat quietly. In front of me wasn't Yu Huixian, the Yu Huixian who had been won over by so many men, but rather a lonely, tired, half-old silhouette of a woman.

Nobody sympathized with the old worn-out rouge on her cheeks.

Nobody sighed for her sighs.

After 'The Last Rose of Summer' faded away from the strings, she sighed for a moment and said, 'Do you know that tune? A very familiar very familiar old tune.'

'I really like that tune.'

'I simply love that tune more than any other. When I was six years old, one summer night, my mother taught me this song; I still remember this song, though my mother died a long time ago. I taught this song to Shaoming, I still remember this song, but what about Shaoming? I taught this song to many people, but now they are all strangers to me. This song survives along with all of my memories . . .'

I was listening to this half-old woman telling me her story—on the table, there were two glasses of liquor. While dancing, her face pressed against my shirt; at the door of the dance hall, she hung on my arms; in the car on the way home, she leaned against my shoulder.

The late spring night was truly on the hot side. I opened the window, stood at the seventh-floor window, looked out at the street scene melting in the lights. The midnight city had fallen deeply asleep. Only a pair of neon eyes was looking at me from under the sky-blue sheets. I pulled out the half-full carton of Craven 'A' cigarettes that she had put in my pocket and had a smoke. A faint fog of smoke floated into the void of the night, and two illusions floated before my eyes.

One was a half-old, tired, lonely woman, unidentifiable, gravely looking at me.

One was a young, childlike girl laughing merrily.

Again I thought of Haowen's words, and the coldly smiling eyes of Miss Lin . . . Lonely!

Every day with a new man, wasting her youth amid the jazz music: all the men love her, but none of the men love her—I felt lonely for her.

> But I love her, because she has an old heart, encased in a young body.
>
> 21st

On the second day we came out of the cinema, in the car:
'And I love you!' I whispered.
'Do you also want to be my gigolo?'
'And why not be your lover?'

'I won't love one man. If you've bumped into me for the first time, you tell me: "I love you!" And then I say: "We've only just met, give me a few days then I'll love you." If we've been lovers for a month, you tell me: "I love you!" And I say: "I won't love you any more." If we've been lovers for a year, you tell me: "I love you!" And I say: "I don't know you."'

I took a turn, and drove onto a remote street.

'You will love "me".'

'No I won't.'

'Yes, you will, because I love you.'

'No man can sincerely and enduringly love a woman—'

Suddenly she grabbed my arm and pulled it tightly: 'Do you remember Norma Shearer's expression from the movie just now?'

I turned my head, and saw her lift her head slightly, her eyes were shining with an intoxicating light: 'Look, is it this?' Her eyelashes slowly covered the top half of her eyelids.

I hit the brakes, and when I turned off the headlights, I discovered a slightly trembling mouth underneath my chin. 'Remember, afterwards the man embraced her.' Then I kissed that trembling cherry.

She whispered in my ear, 'You bad thing!'

'Let me perform for you as well.'

'Call me every day, you bad thing!'

'Why?'

'Because you are my gigolo, you bad thing!'

'You are a bad thing!'

'Black Cat, do you really love me?'

'Really.'

'I don't believe you, you are a bad thing!'

II

The night wind was blowing a requiem. Looking down from above, two rows of streetlights stretched out unbroken and without end, and the headlights of the cars were interweaving like searchlights in the oceanic night. The night-time metropolis was floating on the ocean of darkness, nebulous, pastel-like.

The tips of the large moon were hooked upon the broad leaves of a palm tree, and in front of the trunk bearing its brown fur were couples of men and women. Around the music stage was gaudy red and showy green, with a forced background and primitive tone. Around wildfires of the neon lights were sitting a tribe of earthy people—the fast-beating snakeskin drum made one's stomach vibrate and shake. Clapping hands, blowing trumpets, yelling, as if in fear that wild animals were coming out of the forest to attack. Under the Japanese-style paper lanterns were a group of people cut off from civilization, throwing themselves into the feeling of the barbaric music, and searching for stimulation of their nerve endings.

Following the beat of the rhumba, swaying her head and shoulders like a pendulum, Craven 'A' was dancing, her hair spreading outward like a parasol, in the arms of Little Moustache. Little Moustache's head was all sweaty with fatigue, he was breathing heavily and laughing merrily. I was waving a big palm-leaf fan, looking at this black African woman:

'You are dancing so wildly!'

Looking as if the earth itself was about to sink down into the depths.

Qianping was suddenly at my side saying, 'You're not allowed to look at her!'

'And why is that?'

'That kind of person!'

A woman wearing a black *qipao* hurriedly walked over and stood beside me, staring towards the middle of the hall, with an angry look on her face.

'Look, this is Little Moustache's wife, there's going to be a show on!' Qianping perked up.

This woman spotted Little Moustache, and steaming with anger she went in and separated them, then she slapped Craven 'A' in the ear just above her cheek.

'Hussy! You shameless hussy!'

At my side, Qianping started clapping her hands. I saw many women at their tables laughing.

'Maybe they want to lift Little Moustache's wife above their heads and parade her around like a national heroine'—thinking this, I left the happy Qianping at the table side and walked over, and saw Little Moustache lowering his head. Craven 'A' had already run outside into the hallway.

I rushed outside to the hallway just in time to see her jump into an elevator. I made it into the elevator, and when she saw me, like a collapsed building she fell into my arms and began to cry, like a child who'd been mistreated.

Fifth floor, fourth floor, third floor, second floor--we plummeted downward.

'Shall we go get a drink?'

'Fine, child.'

Coming out of the hotel, her hair was covering her eyes, and her mouth had the sweet scent of grape wine. Her unrouged cheeks were also red. I stuffed the cigarette butt in my pocket, and got into the car.

In the car, she was laughing loudly.

'One cat, two dogs,' she was talking like this.

'It was like, when I was seventeen years old . . . he said, love, have another drink . . . it was like . . . you know? . . . my heart was pounding that hard . .'

(She pulled my hands and pressed them onto her chest.)

'It was like, he carried me onto the bed, I didn't know anything . . . I wasn't drunk today, I could still talk . . . the next day came, and I found that I was sleeping on the bed in a hotel, my virginity torn away like a ripped sheet of paper . . .'

Her head leaned against my shoulder, and slowly she stopped making any more sound, like a melted snowman. On my shoulder was a sleeping child. In the midst of a dream she was sleep-talking: 'I was crying . . . he didn't say anything . . . yes . . . he didn't say anything . . . after, I didn't see him any more . . .'

When the car stopped in front of my apartment, she was already out of speech, and quietly sleeping on my arm. I carried her out of the car, and draped her arm on my shoulder, carried her inside the door. The Indian door guard was smiling at me. I carried her into the elevator, and underneath a crookedly worn black soft felt hat with the three characters for 'driver' embroidered in gold, the elevator man was smiling at me. We went to the door of my apartment room, and the attendant, bowing as he opened the door, suddenly cocked his head and smiled at me. When I'd entered into the room, the door was locked with a click. I understood those smiles and understood the clicking sound of the key.

By the time I put her on the bed, my shirt was already soaked through with sweat.

Lying on the bed was a mannequin displayed inside the shop window of a women's accessory store. The red flowers imprinted on the breast were blooming in the heat of the June night inside the flower room of a bachelor pad, imparting a hot scent. Was this a living creature or a non-living creature? With nightfall, the mannequin was also naked. It was already midnight! And like a well-practised shop window dresser, I removed the mannequin's accoutrements. High heels, black leather belt—the tailoring of modern clothing was so complicated! While admiring the skills of the tailor, I loosened fifty buttons, and finally I succeeded in pulling all the clothing off the mannequin.

Was this a living creature or a non-living creature?

This wasn't a mannequin, nor was it a marble statue, nor a snowman; this was some fluid strands transplanted from a painting, a pile of cream painting a person on my bedsheet.

Having unbuttoned the buttons of eight thick, tight belts, I peeled away a layer of silky dream, and then I saw two white snakes crossed over each other, the undergarments and the thick, tight belts hung down below the hips, wrapping around her. A pink corset tightly bit into her breasts—no need to take off any more clothing, the corset was just another part of her skin? I felt the alcohol I'd just imbibed coming up from below. And then I realized that I already wasn't the window dresser, but rather a traveller on an 'express' journey around the country. Then I saw my own hands venture onto the fertile plain, slowly climbing up the small twin mountains. On the stone tablet on the mountaintop I left some writing and, following the declivity, headed for the great trading port. She suddenly turned her body, and murmured a couple of phrases. Then she turned back over again, pursing her lips a bit, like a child. 'Completely childlike!'—while thinking about how she had looked in the elevator at the dance hall, when as soon as she saw me she collapsed into my arms sobbing. Leaning on me like that!

I covered her with a layer of blankets, and washed my face in cold water, acting as her father, acting as her brother. I ran out and turned off the light, sat on the sofa, and without taking off my clothes, I slept. I had a night of dreams: dreaming I was on an airplane; dreaming I'd sprouted wings, sitting on an airplane flying upward; dreamed I was ice-skating; after that, I dreamed that I was sliding down a mountaintop, and a moment later I was in deep slumber. Later I had other dreams, dreamed that a mosquito flew into my nose, itching like hell, I used my finger to pry it out, and it flew out, I put down my hand, and it flew back in—afterwards, I opened my mouth and sneezed, opened my eyes, and saw a pair of eyes smiling at me wickedly. She was crouching in front of me, her hand holding a thin piece of paper, her hair still tousled.

'Bad thing!' I said, scratched my nose and yawned.

'Did you sleep here the whole night?'

'Didn't I give the bed to you to sleep in?'

'Wasn't it you who took off my clothing?'

'I unfastened fifty or more buttons!'

'Why didn't you remove my underwear and corset, and put on some pyjamas? See, wouldn't that be easy? Just open it from here and you're done. You made me sleep uncomfortably the whole night.'

'If it were other guys, they would have removed them from the start. See, I was on the sofa the whole night.'

'Sweetie!' Suddenly she cupped my face and kissed me, told me to close my eyes, and once more I fell deep asleep. After I woke up, she was gone.

The night returned, and somehow I couldn't feel the key in my pocket, so I called the attendant to open my door. The room was bathed in moonlight, making the window netting so bright and clear, framing a tranquil star field, and the bed was shadowed in a lovely way. I didn't feel like turning on the lights, changed into my pyjamas, and smoked a cigarette in the darkness, watching the moonlight move onto the bed, shining on half of it. I walked to the bedside and laid myself down, one hand reached over to pull the blanket, and touched a person's body, which scared me so that I jumped up, only to feel the grip of an arm. In the darkness was a body as bright as the window netting, without corset or underwear.

'I didn't get drunk today. I've been waiting here for a long time.'

'So it was you who took my key this morning?'

I lay down again, and yesterday's liquor came up from below.

III

I ate breakfast and sat in front of the window reading the newspaper. Suddenly I received a woman's voice on the phone. 'It's probably another divorce case?'—so thinking I picked up the receiver.

'Attorney Yuan's office.'

'You scared me to death, Attorney Yuan's office!'

'Who are you?'

'You know who I am?'

I recognized her—this was the crisp, orange-scented voice of Craven 'A'.

'It's you?'

'Why don't you come see me?'

'Oh . . . ummm . . . I . . .' I'd almost forgotten about her, because recently I'd taken on three contentious inheritance cases, and I was extremely busy.

'Don't . . . Oh . . . ummm . . . me, just come over!'

'If you give me a kiss through the phone, then I'll come.'

From inside the receiver came a *tsss* sound, followed by a laughing sound, and then it was cut off—and when I spoke again, there was nobody on the line.

(*tsss tsss tsss tsss tsss*)

This sound rang like thunder in my head. I followed the address she'd written down for me, and walked over to a quiet little street in the French Concession. I found number 58, it was a small French-style house. I went up to it and rang the doorbell. One of the windows on the right-hand side opened, and a head emerged out of the green window shade.

'Mi . . . !' she called imitating a cat, and blew a stream of smoke onto me.

I walked to the window, and she disappeared behind the green window shade. Leaning on the window I yelled, 'Huixian!'

'Mi . . . !' She was standing gracefully at the door, wearing a suit, the round collar blown up by the morning breeze.

When I walked to the door, she took me by the hand, and extremely delighted we jumped inside the living room. It was a very simple setting, with one long sofa, two easy chairs, a round table, a fireplace, a small tea table, a futon on the floor, a wireless radio, a white cat lying on the tiles by the fireplace, sticking out its tongue in the heat. Sunlight leaked into the room through the green window shade, lighting up the base of a grandfather clock. It was a quiet June morning. I sat down on the easy chair:

'How are you? Happy?'

She moved the futon over to me, and sat childlike below my legs, lifting her head, and parrot-like she spoke these words: 'Really lonely. It's summer again, such a long summer! You see, everyone is gone, and I'm here at home alone smoking a cigarette. Lonely! I constantly feel it. Do you have that feeling as well? A kind of bone-cutting loneliness, as vast and deep as the ocean, welling up from the spine, which cannot be washed away by tears or sighs, nor comforted through love or friendship—I fear it! I feel as if I'm standing on this planet alone, and I've been cut off from all society.

Such loneliness. Have I grown old? I'm only twenty! Why should I have such a feeling of loneliness and isolation?'

'So this is why you had so many gigolos?'

'Gigolos? Yes, I have many. Look!' She took a photo album from the table and handed it to me, and then she ran out.

I opened the thick photo album: the photos were all of smiling men wearing ties. I was thumbing through it, when she came running over with an exquisite little silver box, a glass of fresh orange juice, and a box of candies: 'Look at what's inside this silver box.' Inside the silver box were handkerchiefs and letters: on those faded silks and yellowed paper letters, hearts and characters written in blood.

'So many people! Some said, if I didn't love them they would take their own lives, some said that they were preparing to be lifetime bachelors, some said they were prepared to hate all of the women in the world . . . But those who said they'd take their own lives are still living in good health, and to everyone they say: "So cheap! Was she really worth taking my own life for?" Those who would remain lifetime bachelors have already had children; those who said they'd hate all women are now maniacally chasing other women around, but they say: "I loved wrongly once, how could I have fallen in love with such a cheap woman!" Men all have lying mouths, and they won't come to see me any more. They say that I played around with them—was it not them who played around with me? *Pi!* . . . So lonely! I can only twist my hair, sitting here silently, smoking cigarettes.' Like a child that had been mistreated, she leaned against my knees, pouting her lips.

'Good child, I still love you!' I said, patting her head.

'I don't believe you.' Suddenly she turned her head, kneeling on the floor looking at me, pulling on my collar: 'Truly? Truly?'

'Truly.'

Then she stood up straight, her arms wrapped around my neck, and pulled my head down: 'Truly?' She hung her entire body on my neck, rocking my shoulders back and forth: 'Really truly? Truly?'

I kissed her gently on the lips: 'Truly!'

Without moving at all, she looked intently into my eyes.

'You don't believe me?'

She lowered her arms, and suddenly as if she'd stopped breathing, she collapsed on my legs, her spine resting against my knees: 'I don't believe you. They say I'm cheap! Cheap! They say I'm cheap!' A dark loneliness fluttered across her face, she no longer made any sound, as if she were fast asleep.

Her legs stuck out in front, the two black-mouthed gulls beneath her feet, silently.

I understood this lonely heart.

"The Last Rose of Summer" from her mouth, also sounding like it was leaking out from the gulls' mouths, like sighing.

> *No rosebud is nigh,*
> *To reflect back her blushes*
> *Or give sigh for sigh.*

IV

In order to solve the three big inheritance cases, I was busy for over a week, and I also travelled to Nanjing one time. On the way to Nanjing, at the train station I telephoned her—I wanted to tell her that upon my return I'd pay her a visit. I didn't expect that, after five phone calls, the person kept telling me that their family name was Xia, so I recited the phone number to them, and asked them if this was the number.

'Yes. It is 38925.'

'Is this Yu of the French Concession?'

After a moment the person answered: 'Yes, who are you looking for?'

'I'm looking for Huixian. Sorry, please ask your Miss to come answer the phone.'

'We don't have someone like that here.' Then the connection dropped.

At the time, I was in a hurry to catch a cab, and didn't call again. After returning from Nanjing, I saw a letter on the table in my apartment—it had been mailed out two days before. I opened it up: inside was a key, along with a small white paper.

> Black Cat:
>
> I've gone. I believe that in this world, only you will remember me!
>
> Craven 'A'

I sat down, and took out a Craven 'A' from on the table and smoked it, from the smoke came floating an image, a tired, lonely, half-old woman's image.

> *'Tis the last rose of summer*
> *Left blooming alone.*

After I'd smoked it, I then took the key and put it in a little wooden box as a memento. I prepared to make another key.

2 February 1932

Note

1. A Shanghai delicacy.

4

Night

夜 (1933)

'Night', the briefest in this selection of Mu's short stories, begins with the universal figure of a sailor arriving in Shanghai on the Huangpu River, majestically painted in brief strokes by the synaesthetic vision of Mu. The sights, sounds and smells of a hazy evening on the river swirl around us as we enter into the experience of the sailor, who watches from the deck as his outfit billows around him. He appears as a sort of transcendent figure, a ghost in the Shanghai night. The identity, name and nationality of the sailor are left unspecified. The sailor thus takes on a transnational quality, which is emphasized by the ongoing theme in the story of 'home', or lack thereof.

While the sailor has travelled to many exotic places and sampled the flavours, cuisine and women of various ports and towns around the world, he is fundamentally a 'homeless' person. Upon arriving in the city, as most sailors tend to do, he sets out on a journey to assuage his loneliness, eventually finding himself in a cabaret. One assumes that the cabaret is one of the low-life joints that infamously lined the short alleyway known as Blood Alley, or possibly the more dangerous zone of the Trenches in Hongkou, where bars frequented by soldiers and sailors from all over the world vied for patrons with their Russian, Eurasian, Indian, Japanese and Chinese hostesses.

Once ensconced in the lively environment of the cabaret, with sailors dancing to an exotic 'southern' beat, the protagonist spots a woman sitting alone, who seems to be holding a mirror up to him. Like him, she is lonely, and appears as a pathetic figure. The bar girl or dance hostess figure in this story thus reminds us of many of the night-time workers in Mu's world of Shanghai dance halls, such as the Black Peony, or even in some respects Craven 'A', who are nursing their loneliness while rapidly and inevitably aging their way out of the young world of dance hall hostesses.

It should be noted that most hostesses started in the profession at the age of sixteen or seventeen, and, by the age of twenty, they were on their way out—either they married or else they found another job in the city's night-time demi-monde. The excessive drinking, smoking, coffee consumption, dancing and merriment of hundreds of long nights, and the constant exchange of male partners both on and off the dance floor must have had a deleterious effect on the constitutions and psychological states of these women. As the story progresses, the sailor and the girl engage in a brief conversation followed by dancing, and end up sharing a room for the night. Little is said by either, and much is assumed about their respective lifestyles, but a connection is made nonetheless. This is a terse depiction of a 'one night stand', in our contemporary parlance, ending on an ambiguous note. Has the sailor found the girl of his dreams? Perhaps, but more likely Mu is reminding us how illusory true love can be.

Night

No sorrows, and no joys—an emotional vacuum.

Yet, then where to go?

The river water slapped the shore with a *walla walla* sound, and returned as a mouthful of white foam. The night sky was dark blue, the moon large, within the heart of the river the reflection of the moon was distorted and angular. From Pudong to Puxi, on the surface of the river, the moonlight was reflected for miles, as if the moon were carried by the sterns of the boats. A small sampan rowed over in the moonlight—the oarsman had silvery hair.

The sound of the Customs Building bell floated over the watery surface.

The wind was blowing, blowing on the collar of the sailor, as he tossed a cigarette butt into the water.

The May night, gently, gently . . .

Always like this from port to port, wearing his sailor's cap at an angle, letting the wind blow on his collar, bell-bottomed pants swaying, like a wandering night spirit, strolling alone in the night-time metropolis. He'd heard young girls singing songs for selling coconuts in a forest of coconut trees in Cuba, he'd seen a Carmen with a silk scarf and a red flower above her black temples

Shanghai's New Customs House

Figure 13

From Peter Hibbard's personal collection.

Figure 14
From Peter Hibbard's personal collection.

in the narrow streets of Madrid, he'd supped tea with Madame Chrysanthème inside a tiny teahouse in Kobe, but he was lonely.

A sailor, gypsy of the seas. Where is home? Home!

Shall we go? So he walked, lazily. Pairs of men and women were strolling on the sidewalk, in a streetcar a small-framed girl sat amidst big sailors, a rickshaw puller with a huge grin asked him if he wanted to play with girls, he could take him there . . .

No sorrows, and no joys—an emotional vacuum.

Was it truly an emotional vacuum?

Let's get something to drink! Drunk people are happy—isn't Shanghai the kingdom of happiness?

He turned a corner and walked into a cabaret.

The stimulating odour of alcohol, slumped shoulders and crouching dance of sailors, the drum beat of a tattoo from the sultry southern latitudes, all of the liquor glasses and bottles spread out on the floor, limpid yellow liquor, air thick with sexuality—all of these familiar and intimate old companions. But the laughter of a crude drunken lout was a bit too raucous!

He sat down at the table, drinking his wine. He was familiar with the scent of the liquor, as intoxicating as a night in May. A big horn repeatedly blew:

> *I know there will be a day,*
> *I will find her, find her,*
> *the lover of my wandering dreams.*

The dancing people were melting in the music as if they had lost their souls. He also desired to melt into the scene, yet he alone felt that he could not flow into there, but only stand there frozen, because he had a fossilized heart and an emotionless vacuum.

There have been some girls that I've forgotten long ago,
Forgot her like a touch of sunset glow at dawn;
Some still remain in my memory—
On the face of the water, in the smoke, on a flower,
She keeps saying to me:
'Have you seen? I'm here.'

Because he had a fossilized heart and an emotionless vacuum, because he was drinking alone, because drinking alone was dull, because there was no girl to keep him company . . .

There was a girl sitting at the table to his right, with half a cup of coffee. She wore a black Chinese gown, with a wide belt. Looking from the side, she had a high nose, delicate corners of her mouth, long brows and a face without make-up, her chin rested on her hands, in a fragile way. Her hair and heels were lonely.

He took a deep drag and tossed the burning butt of his cigarette in front of her, and when she turned her head, like a practised old hand, he put his thumb on the side of his nose, and nodded to her:

'Hello, baby.'

He stood up and sauntered over to her. She only stared coldly at him, a face with no expression. Her eyes were full of sensual depravity, her mouth had too much smoke, and was a bit crooked.

'Are you alone?'

She didn't make a sound, took the coffee and had a sip. From her style of drinking coffee, he could tell that she was a person who neither loved life nor hated it. But her look was jaded.

'Who are you waiting for?'

He pulled out his smokes, and handed her one. She took the cigarette, without saying a thing, lit it, had a puff, blew out the smoke, blew out the match. While breaking the matchstick, she looked at the cigarette in her hand, and slowly:

'I'm waiting for a man like you.'

'You look very lonely it seems.'

'Don't I? I always look very lonely.' She laughed tepidly, and in a moment her laughter disappeared.

'Why? Isn't there laughter and good booze here?'

She regarded him from amid the smoke.

'And also wild music! But why do you also seem very lonely!'

He just stood up and pulled her along, making for the big horns, dancing. Dancing: There were so many people here, such bright shiny clothing, such fragrant whisky, such cute girls, such a gentle melody, everyone had smiles on their faces, but the smiles seemed to be forced.

A drunkard slipped suddenly, and everyone started to laugh. He'd just lifted himself up when he fell again onto the floor. He grabbed somebody's legs, lifted his head and asked:

'Where's my nose?'

His buddy lifted him up, and he was holding his nose and crying.

The sailor heard her laughing in his arms.

'I didn't imagine that I'd meet you tonight, I've been searching for a girl like you for a long time.'

'Why are you searching for a girl like me?'

'I love a tired and vulnerable look, lips that have been kissed by many men, black eyes, a jaded spirit . . .'

'You've been to many places?'

'Wherever there is water I have been, I am home wherever I roam.'

'And you've loved many women, right?'

'But I'm searching for a girl like you.'

'So you look very lonely.'

'So you also look very lonely.'

He held her a little more closely, she pressed against his body, and lifted her head, looking at him quietly. He didn't understand the look in her eye. Behind her transparent look was hidden a vast ocean of secrets, twenty years of wandering. Yet he loved that kind of look, he loved things that were beyond his comprehension.

They returned to the table and he looked at her across the liquor glasses.

'Where do you live?'

'Why are you asking that!'

'Can you tell me your name?'

'Why ask that! I have too many names.'

'Why won't you tell me anything?'

'As if after tonight, we are likely to ever meet again? As long as you remember that there's a girl like me, it'll be fine, why must you know who I am?'

> *I know there will be a day,*
> *I will find her, find her,*
> *the lover of my wandering dreams.*

He raised his head and drained his glass, and his heart was lifted. She was really a lovely girl. All of a sudden, somebody tapped his shoulder.

'Buddy, have you seen my nose?' It was that drunkard.

'You left your nose at home, you didn't take it out with you.' The liquor was still in his throat, and when he was tapped it made him start coughing.

'Home? Home?' The drunkard started laughing, staring at the girl, stretched out his hand and lifted her chin: 'Can you guess where my home is?'

She lazily pulled his hand away.

'I'll tell you, my home is inside my nose, today I left my nose at home, I forgot to take it with me.'

The drunkard's buddy had just run over to pull him back and, hearing his friend, he started laughing. A girl at the table to the left of them was so humoured by him that her drink all came spraying out of her mouth. But she lifted her head and looked at him piteously, as if he were a motherless child. His leg was so wobbly that he could barely stand up, and he was propped up by his buddy.

'Let's go home.'

'OK. See ya later!' He gestured with his arm, and then—'I'm going back home, back home!' he sang. Clapping his hands he ran into the crowd of dancers, bumping into other people, and bumping into them he barked out orders: *Attention! Salute!* In a moment he was out of sight, but his voice could be heard, over the sounds of the horns and laughter.

'I'm going back home, back home, back home!' Loud, monotonous and crude, like the sound of a broken record player.

She sighed quietly.

'We are all homeless people!'

Where was home? Home!

There were no horns, no reeds, no cymbals, no big drums, only a small violin softly playing a melancholy tune. He thought about the dawn of that day, leaning against the coconut tree in Hawaii, playing a mouth harp, watching the vast ocean and hazy sun.

Yet another gentle sigh. She had an indefinable look in her eyes, that of a sufferer of weak nerves, dispirited yet pleasing. But then again her face had a coldness to it that he just couldn't understand.

'It seems that I've seen you somewhere before.'

'I also feel that I've seen you somewhere before, but I can't think where.'

They drank silently. One glass, two glasses, three glasses . . . there are some days when alcohol doesn't salve one's worries. His face reddened, but his heart grew heavier.

'When it's possible to be happy, then just be happy for a spell.'

She suddenly stood up, one hand resting on his shoulder, and led him onto the dance floor, stepping lively, turning, placing her arm around his waist as if to lead him—smiling at him, she made a face and started dancing the tango. She spun around a few times and returned to his embrace, stepping backward and bending her waist, then spinning outward, and leaning back over his arms, her left hand climbing his chest.

The big slow drum went *dong dong*.

Suddenly her legs went slack, her head leaned against his chest, smiling.

'I'm drunk.'

'Find a place to sleep.'

Her entire body was already leaning on his body, and was getting heavier. Heading out the door, her eyes closed and a big smile hung from her mouth. In the night wind of May, her clothing was thin. But the May night, gentle . . . gentle.

There was nobody on the street, silently they walked, walked.

Arriving at a hotel, he placed her on the bed, extinguished the light, in the darkness he stood in front of the window smoking a cigarette. The moonlight streamed in from the window, on the floor, resembling a cube of water. The azure smoke flew out the window in curls, dissolved slowly in the night air, then was gone.

'Give me a cigarette.'

He took out a cigarette and gave it to her. She lit it and started puffing away. The burning tip of the cigarette sparkled and shone.

Lying flat on the bed, her arm rested under her head, and her face was pale.

He walked to the bed, put one foot on the bed, stared at her—she was just staring at the ceiling. He spit his cigarette butt onto the floor, wrapped her in an embrace, and without a word he planted a kiss on her lips. Under his face he saw a pair of eyes, cold and indifferent. She pushed his face away, took a drag of the cigarette, and laughed. Taking the cigarette butt, she pulled on his ear and blew smoke into his mouth. Then she patted him on the cheek. He carried her over to the mirror, and breathed onto the surface, and in the fog of this breath he used his finger to draw a heart. She also breathed onto the mirror and drew a heart, and then drew an arrow that pierced through both hearts, connecting them. Then she took her face powder and puffed it over the hearts, and with a flick of the wrist she puffed some on his face.

'Big baby!'

She laughed as she said this, put her arms around his neck, pressed her face against his, her two legs dangling from his arms. Suddenly he felt his face warming up. Looking at her, he discovered that her eyes were full of tears.

'What is it?'

'Where are you going tomorrow?'

'I don't even know, I just have to go wherever the ship takes me.'

'But what's the use of talking about it? Tomorrow is tomorrow!'

Behind the tears was a smiling face, kissing him passionately.

He awoke and raised his body, looked at the girl lying there next to him, and thought about the previous night. Two high-heeled shoes were strewn on the floor by the bed. He looked at his wristwatch, which he hadn't removed, but it had stopped.

Lightly he climbed out of bed, smoked a cigarette and put on his clothing. He took some money out of his pocket, and put half of it next to her pillow. Then he put some cigarettes down next to the money, turned around and saw the mirror—on the mirror were two hearts connected with an arrow—then he put the rest of the money on the pillow, whereupon she awoke and opened her eyes.

'Going?'

He nodded his head.

She looked at him, again with that jaded, cold expression.

'What about you?'

'I don't know.'

'What are you going to do later?'

'I don't know.'

'Will we have a chance to meet again?'

'I don't know.'

She lit a cigarette.

'See you again.'

She sighed *a-i*, and said: 'Remember my name, I'm Yindi.'

He then left, singing to himself:

> *I know there will come a day,*
> *when I will find you, find you,*
> *the girl of my wandering dreams.*

5

Shanghai Fox-trot
上海的狐步舞 (1934)

'Shanghai Fox-trot' is Mu's best-known story and, in some ways, his most accomplished one. This story brings together many of the writer's stylistic qualities to produce a panoramic moving picture of Shanghai during its heyday as the Paris of the Orient. The story moves along at a frantic clip, mirroring the fast-paced life of the modern city.

Mu begins at the city's outskirts, where a gangland killing is taking place. Judging from the newspapers of the times, this would have been a common occurrence out on the western edge of the city, the area known as Huxi, which also became known as 'the Shanghai badlands' for all of the gang violence that took place there. We are then carried along by a train, which Mu connects with the city's cabaret culture through the sound of the wheels as it speeds along.

If there are three main characters in the story, they are the well-to-do Mr. Liu Youde ('has virtue' is a translation of his given name) and his ne'er-do-well son, Xiaode ('little virtue'). Father and son both share the affections of a concubine in an incestuous relationship, which may not have been that uncommon given the tendency of older men to choose young women from Shanghai's demimonde as their 'little wives' (*xiao laopo*).

After borrowing money from his dad, the son drives with the concubine into town to 'kick it up' in a cabaret. As the headlights of the car shine on the streetlamps, Mu turns them into a chorus line of dancers' legs. As the night progresses, the story becomes more and more dreamy, tangled and disjointed, much as a night on the town involving dancing, bar-hopping and copious amounts of alcohol might feel. The cabaret takes on the qualities of a Chagall painting, with dancers 'floating in air' as they waltz to the music. Mu certainly would have been most welcome in Paris during the same age!

An elevator then whisks the reader down to street level, into the chaos and cacophony of one of Shanghai's great thoroughfares. We are exposed to construction workers, shedding their blood to build the phantasmagoric infrastructure of the modern metropolis, to beggars and street urchins, student demonstrators and prostitutes. Mu himself appears in a cameo role as a writer who is lured into an alleyway by a would-be-procuress, trying to earn money off her daughter-in-law's body. The stream-of-consciousness passages that emanate from the writer's mind are none other than Mu's own thoughts as he strolled along the city's fairways, much like the flaneur of Baudelaire's age.

The story ends with a call to awaken from the illusory world of nighttime pleasures, just as Mu's German-Jewish contemporary, Walter Benjamin, urged his fellows to awaken from the phantasmagoric lures of the modern capitalist metropolis.

Shanghai Fox-trot

Shanghai. A heaven built upon a hell!

Huxi, a large moon climbs the sky, shines over a vast field. Ashen field, blanketed with silver-grey moonlight, inlaid with deep-grey shadows of trees and row upon row of farmhouses. On the field, steel rails draw a bowline, following the sky out to the horizon.

Lincoln Road. (Here, morality is trampled underfoot, while evil is uppermost on the mind.)

Gripping a food basket, he walks alone, one hand in pants pocket, watching his hot breath escape his mouth and float slowly into the azure night.

Three human shadows wearing black silk robes and jackets appear before him. Three faces, only noses and chins visible under their hats, block him.

'Go slowly, pal!' they say.

'Got something to say, then say it, *amigo!*' he replies.

'As the old saying goes, "Every injustice has its origins, every debt its creditor." We ain't got nothing against you, but every man has to answer to his boss. We need to eat too, so don't take this personally. Next year this day will be your anniversary, remember!'

'That's a laugh! Not that we aren't friends—' Tossing his food basket, with one hand he grabs the guy's gun and belts him a good one.

Bang! The hand lets go, the man falls down, clutching his stomach. *Bang!* Another shot.

'Punk! The nerve!'

'See you again next life, pal!'

Black Silk Gown takes the pile of hats, shelves them on his head, crosses the steel rails and is gone.

'Help!' The man crawls a few steps.

'Help!' He crawls another few steps.

With a clang, a headlight shines out from beyond the horizon. The steel rail rumbles, its wooden bed crawls forward like a centipede in the light, electricity poles appear then are immediately hidden in the darkness, a 'Shanghai express' pushes out its belly, *ta ta ta*, in the rhythm of the foxtrot, holding its 'night pearl': dragon-like it rushes by, rounding the bowline. It opens its maw with a *kong*, and a trail of black smoke reaches out to its tail—its headlight penetrates the horizon and in a moment is gone.

Again it becomes quiet.

The traffic gate of the tracks interlocks with car headlights. The controller of the traffic gate holds red and green flags, pulls open the white-faced, red-lipped, ruby-earringed traffic gate. Immediately, the cars fly by in a long series.

Onto white painted street tree legs, electricity pole legs, all inanimate legs—like a revue, girls' powdered legs criss-crossing outward . . . A series of white painted legs. Following the quiet avenue, from the windows of houses, like the eyes of the city, penetrating the window shades, seeping out pink, purple, green, everywhere lights.

The car stops in front of a small, Western-style villa and honks its horn. The coral knot on Liu Youde's 'watermelon skin' hat pokes out the car door, out of two pockets of his black velvet waistcoat hangs a gold chain, its gold links tittering, taking him out of the car and carrying him into the house. He tosses a half-finished cigar out the door, and walks into the guestroom. Just as he sits down, the light patter of heels glides down the stairs.

'You've returned?' Vivacious laughter: a woman who in age could be his daughter-in-law but by law is his wife runs into the room, pulls his nose and says, 'Quick! Sign me a cheque for three thousand dollars.'

'You've already used up last week's money?'

She doesn't speak, but hands him a pile of bills, pulls him by his blue gown sleeves into the library, sends a pen into his hand.

'I said . . .'

'What did you say?' She purses her little red mouth.

He stares at her a moment, then signs. She leans down and kisses him on the mouth. 'You can take care of dinner yourself, I'm going out with Xiaode.' Laughing she runs out, and bangs through the door. He pulls out a handkerchief and wipes his mouth. On the kerchief is a Tangee mark. Just like my daughter, all day bothering me for money.

'Pop!'

Xiaode slides in from nowhere, stands at his side, like a rat who's just seen a cat.

'Why have you come back again?'

'Auntie called me to come here.'

'For what?'

'Money.'

Liu Youde finds it funny. These two are up to something.

'Why would she ask you to come back and ask me for money? It's not like she doesn't get enough?'

'It's me who wants money. Auntie asked me to take her out.'

Suddenly the door opens: 'Do you have cash?' Liu Yan Rongzhu runs in again.

'I've only . . .'

A hand that just applied nail polish shoots into his pocket and pulls out his wallet! Red polished nails count out bills: one five, one ten, two tens, three hundreds. 'I'll leave you fifty, and I'll take the rest. If I give you more I'll have to come back.' She casts a seductive glance, then pulls at her lawful son and goes.

The son is a clothing rack. All day he reads fashion magazines meant for a gigolo. He dons a black velvet cape ironed with large folds and broad pleats, a tie knotted in the middle, and escorts his mother by the arm out to the car.

Onto white painted street tree legs, electricity pole legs, inanimate legs—like a revue, girls' powdered legs criss-crossing outward . . . A series of white-painted legs. Following the quiet avenue, from the windows of houses, like the eyes of the city, penetrating the window shades, seeping out pink, purple, green, virginal lights.

Driving a new 1932 Baker, but with a lovers' style of 1980. The deep autumn wind wails, blowing about the son's tie, the mother's hair. Everything feels a bit cold. The lawful mother snuggles into her son's embrace and says:

'It's a pity that you're my son.' Chuckling.

The son kisses the little mouth that his father kissed, and almost drives the car onto the sidewalk. Neon light stretches out a coloured finger and writes a large character in the black-ink night. An English gentleman stands in front, wearing a red swallow-tail coat, gripping a cane, vigorously striding along. Below his feet is written: 'Johnny Walker: Still Going Strong.' By the side of the road on a small plot of grass has opened a real estate company's utopia. Above it an American smoking Lucky brand cigarettes looks on as if to say, 'Too bad this is a small-world utopia. Won't that big field out there give me a foothold?'

In front of the car an individual shadow appears, *honk honk*, the person turns his head and stares and slides out from in front of the wheels and over to the sidewalk.

'Rongzhu, where are we going?'

'To whatever cabaret to kick up a fresh one—I'm sick of the Astor House and Majestic.'

On the rooftop of the horse race-track, a golden horse weathervane seems to kick its legs towards the red moon. Over all directions of the large field of grass shimmers a sea of light, evil waves. The Moore Memorial Church permeates the dark, kneeling, praying for these hell-bent men and women. The Great World tower refuses forgiveness, stares arrogantly back at this priest, flashing its lights.

The azure dusk blankets the whole scene. A saxophone stretches out its neck, opens its great mouth, and blares at them, *Woo woo*. Inside on the smooth floor, floating skirts, floating robes, exquisite heels, heels, heels, heels, heels. Free-flowing hair and men's faces. Men's white-collared shirts and women's smiling faces. Arms outstretched, kingfisher-green earrings dragging on shoulders. A group of tightly arranged round tables, but with scattered chairs. Waiters in white stand in dark corners. Scent of alcohol, perfume, ham and eggs, smoke . . . someone sits alone in the corner holding a coffee to stimulate his energy.

Dancing: the waltz melody enwraps their legs, their legs stand on the waltz melody floating, floating. The son whispers in his mother's ear, 'There are many things that can only be said during

Figure 15

Johnnie Walker whisky advertisement, *North-China Daily News*, 8 December 1934.

a waltz, and you are the greatest waltzing partner—and, Rongzhu, I love you!'

She lightly kisses his temple—mother snuggles into son's embrace, snickering.

A Belgian jewel broker passing himself off as a French gentleman whispers into the ear of movie star Yan Furong, saying, 'Your smile makes all other women in the world envious—that's why I love you!'

She lightly kisses his temple, snuggles into his embrace, snickering. Suddenly she sees that on her finger is another diamond ring.

The jewel broker sees Liu Yan Rongzhu and nods to her over Yan Furong's shoulders, smiling. Xiaode looks back and stares at Yan Furong, lifting his eyebrows like a gigolo.

Dancing: the waltz melody enwraps their legs, their legs stand on the waltz melody floating, floating. The jewel broker whispers into Liu Yan Rongzhu's ear, saying, 'Your smile makes all other women in the world envious—and so, I love you!'

She lightly kisses his temple, snuggles into his embrace, snickering, and puts a lipstick mark on his white shirt.

Xiaode whispers into Yan Furong's ear, saying, 'There are many things that can only be said during a waltz, and you are the greatest waltzing partner--and, Furong, I love you!'

She lightly kisses his temple, and snuggles into his embrace, snickering.

A lone man sits in the corner holding a black coffee to stimulate his energy. Scent of alcohol, perfume, ham and eggs, smoke . . . Standing in dark corners are waiters in white. Chairs are scattered about, but tables are lined up neatly. Kingfisher pendants drag on shoulders, outstretched arms. Women's smiling faces and men's white collared shirts. Men's faces and free-flowing hair.

Exquisite heels, heels, heels, heels, heels. Floating robes, floating skirts, in the midst of a smooth polished floor. *Woo woo*, blaring at them, that saxophone stretches out its neck, opens its big mouth. Azure dawn blankets the whole scene.

Pushing open the glass door, this fragile fantasy world is broken. Running under the steps, a pair of rickshaws stop at the street. The car attendant stands. In the middle is a road lit up by houselights, competing with 'Rickshaw?' are Austins, Fords, Baker sports cars, Baker little nine, eight cylinder, six cylinder . . . the great red-faced moon limps along above the broad field of the race-track. On the street corner, a vendor selling the *Shanghai Mercury* and *Evening Post* uses the voice of a pancake vendor, screaming:

'*Evening Post!*'

An electric tram *dang dang* rides into a dangerous zone, covered with advertisement posters for great big sales and company trademarks. Bicycles are wedged against the side of the tram, looking pitiful. Sailors sit atop the rickshaw, blinking their drunken eyes. Seeing the rickshaw puller miss a step, they laugh loudly, '*Ha ha.*' Red traffic light, green traffic light, traffic light pole and Sikh traffic guard stand upright on the ground. Traffic lights flash and let forth a torrent of people and a flood of cars. These people look like a pack of mindless flies! A fashion model wearing clothes from her shop passes herself off as an aristocratic woman. The elevator speeds along at fifteen seconds per floor, carrying people to the rooftop garden like commodities. A female secretary stands at the display window of a silk shop, staring at a full silk French crepe, thinking of her manager's smiling face scarred by a knife above the mouth. Ideologues and party members holding large propaganda posters stroll by, thinking, if we're caught then we'll make a speech right here. Blue-eyed girls wear narrow skirts, black-eyed girls wear *qipao*. Their hips and legs all have the same feminine charm.

On the side of the road in an empty lot towers a large, pyramid-shaped wooden scaffold, its crudely built legs stuck in the mud, set with a floodlight on the roof, shining downward, shining on every person on the wooden slats on the street. These people yell '*Ai ai ya!*' as atop the roof of the several-hundred-foot-tall wooden structure, wooden pilings fall down, *bang!* Three large, crude wooden columns slam into the mud, floodlights set up in all four corners, the vicious light shines over the entire empty lot. In the empty lot: criss-crossing ditches, steel girders, piles of tiles. Men carrying large wooden columns walk along the ditches, dragging their long shadows. The man in front slips and falls, the wooden column presses down his back. His back breaks, and blood pours from his mouth . . . floodlight . . . *bang!* Wooden pilings flow up the wooden structure . . . a naked child rolls a copper along the tarmac road . . . the floodlight atop the large wooden structure looks just like the moon in the night sky . . . a young woman picks up dregs of coal . . . there are two moons . . . the moon is swallowed up by the astral dog—the moon is gone.

The dead body is carted away. In the empty lot: criss-crossing ditches, steel girders, tiles, and a pool of his blood. On the blood they pour cement, creating the iron infrastructure, and a new hotel is built! A new dance hall is built! A new inn is built! His strength, his blood, and his life are pressed underneath, just like in other hotels, just like the Huadong Hotel that Liu Youde just stepped into.

Inside the Huadong Hotel—

Second floor: white painted rooms, the sweet old coppery smell of opium, mahjong tiles, 'Silang Visits His Mother',[1] 'Courtesan Scolds the Little Whore Tanbai', Old Dragon perfume and the scent of lust, waiters in white, prostitutes and pimps, kidnappers, conspiracies and traps, White Russian vagabonds . . .

Third floor: white painted rooms, the sweet old coppery smell of opium, mahjong tiles, 'Silang Visits His Mother', 'Courtesan Scolds the Little Whore Tanbai', Old Dragon perfume and the scent of lust, waiters in white, prostitutes and pimps, kidnappers, conspiracies and traps, White Russian vagabonds . . .

Fourth floor: white painted rooms, the sweet old coppery smell of opium, mahjong tiles, 'Silang Visits His Mother', 'Courtesan Scolds the Little Whore Tanbai', Old Dragon perfume and the scent of lust, waiters in white, prostitutes and pimps, kidnappers, conspiracies and traps, White Russian vagabonds . . .

The elevator spits him out at the fourth floor. Mr. Liu Youde crooning 'Silang Visits His Mother' strides into a room filled with the sounds of clacking tiles, lights up a cigarette, writes out a summons for a prostitute. In a moment, he is sitting at a table, taking a *zhongfeng*:[2] using well-practised hands he pulls it in, on the one hand saying, 'How is it I can't grab anything good?' with the face of an inveterate gambler, on the other hand listening carefully to the words of Precious Moon Old Number Eight, who because she does not bind her breasts is known as 'Sullivan Bread': 'Sorry, Master Liu, I'm on another summons, in a moment when I'm finished you can come over and sit.'

'Come home with us to sit awhile!' Standing on the street corner, one can only see a stone-grey face with black eyeballs, crouching in the dark corner of a building, yelling at the people going by, like an auctioneer—an old procuress dragging behind like a tail.

'Come home with us to sit awhile!' that ugly mouth is saying, purposely bumping against a flat face. The flat face laughs, and stares awhile, pointing at his nose, searching his brain: 'Would you like to meet a nice old widow, Master?'

'When youthful, friends are important!' Ugly Mouth laughs.

'Never thought that this little Indian sugar baby would be picked up.' Hand rubs her face, then leaves.

On the side a long-haired, unshaven writer is enjoying the spectacle, and he thinks of a topic: 'The second round of pilgrimages—city's dark side pilgrimage sonata.' Suddenly he sees Ugly Mouth's eyes sweep along his own face, and immediately he rushes along.

Stone-grey face crouches in the dark shadows, the old procuress dragging behind like a tail—crouching in the dark shadows a stone-grey face, stone-grey face, stone-grey face . . .

(The writer thinks to himself.)

First round of investigations gambling halls second round of investigations street hookers third round of investigations dance halls fourth round of investigations decide at a later time *Eastern Magazine, Fiction Monthly, Literary Arts Monthly* first sentence write Nanjing Road Beijing Road street hooker meeting place . . . no, that won't do—

Somebody pulls at his sleeve: 'Mister!' He glances around and sees an old woman making a bitter face: she lifts her head and looks at him.

'Whaddya want?'

'Please read a letter for us.'

'Where's the letter?'

'Please come to my house to get it, it's just in this alleyway.'

He goes with her.

China's tragedy here is definitely material for a novel 1931 is my year 'Eastern Fiction' 'Northern Dipper' each month one entry one version translated into Japanese one into Russian one into each language all published Nobel Prize great riches . . .

Pulled into a little alleyway, so dark he can't see a thing.

'Where's your house?'

'It's just here, not far, Mister. Please read a letter.'

There in the alleyway is a yellow street lamp—below the lamp is a girl, head lowered, standing there. The old woman suddenly makes another bitter face, grasps his sleeve and says, 'Mister, this is my daughter-in-law. My son is a mechanic, he stole somebody's belongings, he was caught and taken away, we poor women haven't eaten in four days.'

(Isn't that so? Such good materials skills no problem her speech consciousness surely accurate don't fear them also I'm a humanitarian . . .)

'Mister, have pity, give me some money. I'll let my daughter-in-law stay with you for a night. Save our two lives!'

The writer is shocked. The girl lifts her head; two shadows drag along her emaciated cheeks, the corners of her mouth lift in a smile. The corners of her mouth lift in a smile. A Belgian jewel broker passing himself off as a French gentleman whispers into the ear of Liu Yan Rongzhu, saying, 'Your smile makes all other women in the world envious—have a drink!'

Over a tall-stemmed glass, Liu Yan Rongzhu's pair of eyes are smiling.

In the Baker, those two eyeballs saturated with cocktails are smiling out of tousled hair.

In the hall of the Huamao Hotel, those two eyeballs saturated with cocktails are smiling out of tousled hair.

On the elevator, those two eyeballs are smiling out of purple eye-shadow.

On the seventh floor of the Huamao Hotel inside a room, those two eyeballs are smiling above fiery red cheeks.

The jewel broker discovers those smiling eyeballs under his nose.

Smiling eyeballs!

White bed sheets!

Panting . . .

Panting they lie without moving on the bed.

Bed sheets: melted snow.

'Set up an international club!' Suddenly getting the idea, face sweating in thin trickles.

Sweating, on a quiet street, pulling a drunken sailor into a bar. On the streets, no patrolmen, so quiet, like a dead city. The sailor puts his leather shoe on the rickshaw man's spine, voice echoes in the building walls:

Later . . . later

Later

Later . . .

On the rickshaw man's face, sweat; in the rickshaw man's mind, money rolling, flying and rolling. Drunken sailor suddenly jumps down, disappears into two glass doors.

'Hello, Master! Master!'

So crying he chases him to the door. A Sikh patrolman holds his club out and blocks his way, laughter squeezes out the door, aroma of alcohol squeezes out the door, jazz squeezes out the door . . . the rickshaw man pulls his rickshaw along, battering him is the river wind of December, a cold month, a deep port inside a large building. Thrown out of happiness and fun, he doesn't think of suicide. 'Fuck! Fuck!' he swears aloud, then heads towards life.

Empty, the rickshaw departs, only moonlight on the street. The moon shines on half the street, leaving the other half immersed in darkness. In the darkness crouches that bar, above the door of the bar is a green lamplight, under the green light stands a fossilized Sikh patrolman. He opens the door again and again, like a parrot saying:

'Goodbye, sir.'

Out of the glass door walks a young man, a cane hanging from his arm. He heads out of the light and into the darkness, then from out of the darkness he walks into the moonlight. He rests a spell, sidles forth—a lover thinking about sleeping in somebody else's bed. He walks along the river, stands by the railing in a daze.

Dawn in the east, sunlight, like a golden eyeball, opens up in the fog.

In Pudong, the high-pitched voice of a man:

'*Ai . . . ya . . . ai . . .*'

Flies up into the sky, together with the first ray of sunlight. Joining him is a chorus of majestic voices. The well-slept buildings stand up, lift their heads, remove their grey pyjamas, the water *walla walla* flows towards the east, factory steam whistles scream.

Singing about a new life, the fate of people in a nightclub!

Wake up, Shanghai!

Shanghai, a heaven built upon a hell!

Notes

1.   A Peking opera tune.
2.   A mahjong tile.

6

Black Peony

黑牡丹 (1933)

'Black Peony' is another of Mu's many studies of the figure
of a dance hostess in Shanghai's cabaret scene, but with
a twist. In this story, the narrator, a man who is 'pressed
down by life' in the modern city, meets a female dancer in
a cabaret who shares his fatigue. In one memorable line, she
claims, 'I'm living in the lap of luxury, if you take away jazz,
fox-trot, mixed drinks, the fashionable colours of autumn,
eight-cylinder engine cars, Egyptian tobacco . . . I become
a soulless person.' This is a woman who is deeply entranced
by and entangled in the material culture of semi-colonial
Shanghai and its effervescent nightlife. After accompanying her through the evening, Mu leaves the reader with a
question: did the narrator also take her home? It is not clear
whether their relationship extends further than a night of
dancing and conversation.

A month later, the narrator receives a letter from a male
friend named Shengwu, who is living in an idyllic retreat
beyond the outskirts of the city. Faced with the enormous
urban sprawl that Shanghai has spawned eighty years after
this story was written, it is easy to forget that the city limits
once extended only to Avenue Haig, now Huashan Road,
where the western borders of the International Settlement
and French Concession then lay. Even Xujiahui, which

is now a bustling district full of department stores, office towers and shopping malls, was then a bucolic landscape of fields and farmlands.

We do not know how far outside the city limits Shengwu lives, but he is in a forested environment that is much closer to 'nature'. The narrator goes to visit his friend and spend the weekend in the 'countryside', only to find that the dancer he had befriended the previous month has also made this place her own retreat. After fleeing a male customer who sought to take advantage of her on a dark road, she has appeared to Shengwu as a mysterious 'peony spirit'. Following a violent encounter with his dog, she settles into his abode. Without questioning her, Shengwu takes her in and makes her his 'wife' (whether they are in fact married or just living together is left unexplained). The story thus gives Mu a chance to explore the virtues of 'simple living' as opposed to the frantic regime of urban life, with its bewildering, transnational flow of people and material cultures. In one fell swoop, the girl herself has been transformed from hostess into Hausfrau.

While not nearly as surreal or disjointed as some of the others in this collection, this story also reflects Mu's synaesthetic bent and his knack for creative wordplay. Naturally, some of this creativity is lost in translation. For example, the measure word in Chinese for flower is duo. Mu uses this same measure word to suggest that her smile is like a flower, 'pinned onto her mouth' just as the carnation is pinned to her temple. He uses the Arabic numeral '3' to suggest ants crawling across the page, just as the trivialities of life accumulate antlike through the lives of his characters. In the end, we find a declaration that is at odds with that of 'Shanghai fox-trot'. The narrator decides to head back into the jazz of urban life, even if he collapses on the roadside!

Black Peony

'I love that one dressed in black, with the thin hips and the tall figure.' My words just flow out of my mouth, rose-coloured cocktail flows from the wheat straw into my mouth, but my eyes flow towards the dancer sitting in front of me.

Above her temple is a white carnation, and when she turns around I see a tall nose and long face, big eyes, slanted eyebrows, the corner of her brow hiding beneath the carnation, long lashes, lips so soft they're oily: beneath the ears hang two pagoda-shaped earrings, hanging down to the shoulders—Spanish style! But it's not these things I love, what I love is the languid way that she sits there, holding her chin, leaning on the table, along with the worn-out flower at her temple, because I'm also a person searching for breath while cast about on the tumultuous tide of life.

As soon as the music begins, from every corner of the dance hall, people rush towards her, and suddenly from behind me passes a man in a tuxedo, and he drags her dancing into the crowd. She dances past me once, twice . . . her face pressed against the sweaty folds of his shirt, supporting her head, languidly watching people from the edge of her carnation. Under the blue light, a thin pair of black satin high-heeled shoes is floating with the rhythm,

Figure 16

An illustration that accompanied the short story 'Black Peony' when it was first published in the Shanghai illustrated magazine *Young Companion* (*Liangyou huabao*) in 1934.

fantastically, like a pair of crows flying beneath a rainbow in the sky. After the fifth time she passes me dancing, 'Neapolitan Nights'[1] fades away under the white lights. One of my eyes sees her sitting down, panting slightly, while the other eye watches 'Tuxedo' walk by me, and on the wrinkles of his stiff shirt is a spot of rouge, while on his chest is a red mark—red looking like what? Only when eating **cream** can you feel that taste.

My spirits rise, and it's like I'm talking in my sleep: 'I love that one dressed in black, she is like a peony fused on the body of a black fox, a mixed-blood child of animal and object.'

She's so enervated that, after each dance, she rests on the table leaning against her cheek.

The wheat straw in her mouth is softening in the alcohol, and when like the line of a fishing pole it floats to the surface of the drink, I take her: her head is bowed in front of mine, her face presses against my shirt. The rouge on her lips goes through my shirt and imprints directly on my skin—and my heart is tainted red.

'You look rather tired,' I say, lowering my head and blowing on her pagoda-shaped earrings.

The earrings dangle . . . the sound of wind chimes blown by the wind atop a pagoda. Below my face, she lifts her face and regards me. What an enchanted, weary look. **S.O.S.! S.O.S.!** In ten seconds I will fall in love with that weary look.

'Why don't you say anything?'

'Pretty tired.'

'Come sit with me at my table.'

After we finish the dance, she grabs her purse and sits at my table.

'You look so tired!'

'I even have a bit of a cold.'

'So why don't you take a day off and stay at home?'

'Rolling in the tide of life, you know, when you want to take a breath, you've already sunk to the bottom of the water and you'll never float back up.'

'Our generation are slaves to our stomachs, slaves to our bodies . . . we are all people crushed by life.'

'Take me, for example, I'm living in the lap of luxury, if you take away jazz, fox-trot, mixed drinks, the fashionable colours of autumn, eight-cylinder engine cars, Egyptian tobacco . . . I become a soulless person. So deeply soaked in luxury, *carpe diem*, I am living this life of luxury, but I am tired.'

'Yes, life is mechanical, moving forward at full speed, but in the end we are all living organisms! . . .'

'There will be a day when we faint from exhaustion halfway down the road.'

'There will be a day when we faint from exhaustion halfway down the road.'

'You are also a tired person!'

'How can you tell?'

'From the way you smile.'

'We should both find a way-station to rest a bit.'

'You got that right!'

She sighs for a moment.

I'm smoking a cigarette.

She's smoking a cigarette.

She is leaning her chin on her hand.

My spine is resting on the back of the chair.

We just sit there like that for half the night, and when the dance hall empties out, we walk together with the happy people out onto the pre-dawn street where a late spring breeze is blowing, and she doesn't ask for my name, and I don't ask for hers. But then I feel that the weight of life that was pressing so heavily upon my back has been lifted greatly, because I've found a person who has been weighed down by life just like me.

One month later, it's a Saturday morning, and I've managed to escape from the red and blue pencils, typewriters, memos, speed-typing, and it's so hot my whole body is dripping with sweat, so I sit down on the bus, my body bumping up and down, looking at the view of the street, thinking, 'This afternoon how should I nurture myself?'—thinking that way, I make plans to go home and take a shower, sleep until five, go to a restaurant and have a sumptuous meal, then hit the dance hall and check out that Black Peony, who like me has been weighed down by life.

At the front entrance to my apartment, the door boy, looking like a tin soldier, opens the door:

'Mr. Gu, you're taking a rest this afternoon.'

'Yes, resting.'

Walking to the elevator, the elevator man opens the elevator door:

'Mr. Gu, what fun do you have planned for this afternoon?'

'Yup, planning on having some fun.'

Out of the elevator, I bump into my neighbour across the hall, a Filipino musician working for the dance hall. He tips his hat:

'It's Saturday!'

'Yup, Saturday!'

So what about Saturday? I don't have any place to go. For a guy like me who's weighed down by life, the universe isn't vast at all.

The floor attendant opens the door for me, and hands me a letter. I unfold the letter:

> Miraculous! Last night in my flower garden, a black peony suddenly blossomed, and standing tall and straight, she smiled at the June wind under the grape arbour. Tomorrow is Sunday, come over to my place for a couple days. At night we can camp out on the grass—you don't know how stimulating a **Sport** camping can be. Come quickly!—
>
> Shengwu, Friday morning

I didn't really feel like sleeping. I took a shower, put on a pair of white golf pants, doffed a cap, and I didn't wear a jacket, then I hopped a cab and drove all the way to Shengwu's villa in the suburbs.

Closing my eyes, I smoked a light cigarette, thinking about his white stone cabana, his flowerbed, the violets growing like a string of pearls on his patio, the fruity scent from his grape arbour.

Shengwu was sort of a hermit. Since the year he graduated from college at the age of twenty-five, he took his not inconsiderable inheritance and settled down here. Every day he'd drink a cup of coffee and smoke a couple of cigarettes. He'd sit on the patio and luxuriate in some novels and gardening manuals. By the evening, he'd sit by himself and listen to the wireless radio, forgetting the world and forgotten by the world, as elegant, gentlemanly and refined as a lambskin-covered book. I envied him. Every time I spent a weekend of leisure at his home, I felt that people who run around frantically in a fast-paced lifestyle are unfortunate. But every Friday that white room held out its hand, smiling, and welcomed me.

When I opened my eyes, I was already on the great big suburban asphalt road. My mood became as carefree and light as a summer outfit. The fields were redolent of over-ripe fruit and the burning aroma of wheat, and all the worries that pressed so heavily upon my lumbar were sent scurrying by a light, ammonia-scented breeze. In the shade of a large tree on the side of a grave-hill, a farmer was lying on his back smoking rolled tobacco. The sound of cicadas in the trees and the sunshine occupied the space of the landscape, and I was in one of Millet's paintings of farms and fields!

The car stopped at a small gravel pathway. I walked along the pathway, turned sharply at the great cypress, and then I saw the little wooden fence and a lawn full of tulips. Shengwu was on the patio. As soon as he heard the barking of his Scottish wolfhound at the fence, he jumped down and ran over. He took my hand and gripped it tightly: 'Old Gu, how are you?'

'You've invited me to see your black peony, eh?'

Suddenly his eyes lit up: 'Black peony? The black peony has become a spirit!'

'Nonsense, surely this is just a daydream you've had from reading *Strange Tales from a Chinese Studio*.'[2]

'Really, shortly I'll explain in great detail, it truly is like a story out of *Strange Tales from a Chinese Studio*. Starting two days ago, I've given up on all scientific rationality.'

We walked into a short wooden tent. The small white room said to me: 'Old Gu, you've come again?'

The mouth of the room opened, and a woman in a black *qipao* came walking out. Carrying a watering can, that face was strangely familiar, seems like I'd seen it before somewhere.

'Look, this is the Black Peony! I invited you here to see the Peony Spirit? Not to see peony flowers.' Yelling, 'Xiao Zhu! Mr. Gu is here!' and pulling me he ran over to the woman.

A Spanish-style long face: above her temple is a white carnation, big eyes, slanted eyebrows, the corner of her brow hiding beneath the carnation, long lashes. Beneath the ears hang two pagoda-shaped earrings, hanging down to the shoulders, lips so soft they're oily . . . (The rouge on her lips goes through my shirt and imprints directly on my skin—and my heart is tainted red.)

'*Ai!*' —I remembered the jaded dancer from a month ago.

She put her finger to her lips. I understood: I subtly nodded my head.

'Mr. Gu, please sit down inside. I'll come as soon as I water the flowers.'

I went inside and sat under the shade of the curtains, drinking a beer brimming with bubbles:

'Shengwu, how did you come to think about marriage?'

'What about marriage?'

'Don't joke with me—'

'What joke? Is it a real Peony Spirit? But I can't tell you the story just now, she'll be back in a moment. Didn't she just press her finger to her lips? She won't allow me to tell a third person what I'll tell you tonight.'

We ate our fill that night, and had our fill of conversation and laughs, under the starry sky. We set up a Sahara Desert tent, and slept on canvas mattresses. I asked him:

'What sort of business is this after all?'

'I'm just ready to tell you, it was the night before last, I was camping out here. That night there was no wind at all, just the sound of mosquitoes buzzing around the four walls of the tent. I was lying on the bed just sweating, above my head was the vastness of a quiet starry sky. I lay down for a spell, and my mind calmed down, I softly recited "A Midsummer Night's Dream", that lively chorus, I was fantasizing about those tulips encircling the black peony and dancing a medieval dance. Suddenly I heard footsteps treading daintily over the footpath, very quietly, as if they were stepping on my dream. I raised myself up and the sound went away. I suspected that I was dreaming. But like a delicate rainfall, *patter! Patter!* In a moment the sound came again! This time I could tell that it was the sound of a woman wearing high heels. A ghost! I opened my eyes and stared, but could only see a figure in black clothing standing at the wooden tent door, amid the darkness. Was it really a ghost? I had just stretched out my hand to grab the flashlight when I heard a howl, as Bob, my wolfhound came bounding over, and jumped out of the tent, then I heard the piercing sound of a shriek emanating from outside, it was the shrill tone of a woman's voice. The figure in black turned around and fled, and Bob went running after her. I grabbed the flashlight and ran outside—Bob had already jumped on her and had her pinned to the ground, without any sound. That really gave me a proper scare—don't crush her to death, this is not a game! Running out hurriedly, yelling at Bob, moving forward, holding the flashlight—I was given a complete shock. Guess who was lying on the ground! A woman with clothing torn in pieces, in the dark, like a marble statue, with eyes closed, shadows of her long lashes covering the lower portion of her eyes, hair spread out on the ground, a white carnation still at her temple, on the white skin of her face and body was flowing blood, one hand holding her breast, blood flowing out from beneath her hand—a very lovely girl! Bob was still holding her down, a growl emanating from his throat, wagging his tail at me, I shooed Bob away, took her in my arms, she suddenly opened her eyes, and panting quietly said, "Carry me inside!" with a pleading look!'

'Who was she after all?'

'Don't rush me, listen as I tell the story. Once inside, I gave her some water to drink, and asked her: "Who are you? How did you come to such a state?" She didn't answer, just asked me where the bathroom was. I told her it was upstairs, and she went up. After an hour or more, she came down again, with a cigarette in her mouth, wearing my pyjamas. She'd washed away the blood, and with the carnation pinned into her dishevelled hair around the temple, and a smile pinned onto her mouth, at that moment she simply entranced me. She went up to me, let out a puff of smoke, and said:

"Why do you raise such a vicious wolfhound?"

"Who are you after all? If you don't explain, I can't let you stay here."

"If you hadn't shown up, I'd really have suspected I was in an African forest, being eaten by a wolf—" Thus, she drew a boundary line around my question.

"So who are you?" I forced her to cut a line through her boundary.

"Look, even here I've been clawed by him!" Suddenly she peeled open her pyjama top, and thrust a scar running from her ripped bra across her breast in front of my face. In the span of a second, all the stars in the sky outside the window collapsed and fell, and in front of my eyes was a bright burning comet's tail. I felt like I was standing atop the line of the equator. "Bandage it for me quickly!"

"I made my mouth into a bandage. After that she became my wife."'

'Then how do you know that she is a Peony Spirit?'

'She told me the next day, every day upon waking, she goes and waters that black peony . . .'

I almost laughed out loud, but then I thought of her putting her finger on her lips that afternoon, and I held back my laugh.

When I awoke the next morning, the canvas mattress beside me was empty, and the sunlight streaming down through the grape leaves was shining so hard that my whole body was drenched in sweat. I lifted my head. Then I saw the Black Peony sitting on the patio quietly smoking a cigarette. Her face didn't have that jaded look any more, the look of being weighed down by life. In the light of the morning sun it was just like the way that Shengwu had described in his letter, 'Standing tall and straight, she smiled at the June wind under the grape arbour.' Her face, amid the worries and joys of life, was much more comely than a month ago.

Thinking about this, I turned over and suddenly I fell off the bed. I got myself up, and she was already by my side:

'Did you sleep well last night?'

'Last night I heard Shengwu tell a story about a Peony Spirit.'

'Really?' She laughed, and pulling me by the arm she went inside. 'Being a Peony Spirit is much more comfortable than being a person.'

'And Shengwu?'

'He goes out for a stroll every morning. Let's eat breakfast first, no need to wait for him.'

I went upstairs and took a shower. By the time I had changed my shirt and came down again, somebody had placed a low table on the patio. On it were two sets of fried eggs, three pieces of toast, a pot of coffee, and sitting opposite to me was one Black Peony.

Next to the coffee pot, those soft, oily lips of hers were chewing on a banana-coloured piece of toast, and spitting out clear and happy words:

'That evening, a dance-hall customer forced me to go with him to the Rio Rita Village,[3] where he pressed me to have mixed drinks. He was singing those pop tunes, and asked the musicians to play the songs he knew I liked, but he was an awful middle-aged man, he took me for a Western doll . . . when he was taking me back home, he purposely chose a wayward route on Zhongshan Road, and when on Columbia Road he suddenly stopped, and seeing the gleam in his eyes I understood. I opened the car door and rushed out; he pulled on my sleeve, and it ripped in an instant. I ran through the fields, and fled across the grasses, and tore through the bushes, shredding all my clothing, and scraping my skin, I didn't dare cry out, worried that he'd catch up with me. By the time I'd completely run out of energy, I'd reached this place, at that fenced path—'

'And after that you bumped into Shengwu?'

'Exactly!'

'But how did you become a Peony Spirit?'

'I fell in love with this room, this place, this quiet, and Shengwu is also a gentleman with the air of a hermit; I was so exhausted, and Shengwu asked me who I was. When I told him that I was a Black Peony Spirit, he believed me. If I'd told him I was a dancer, he wouldn't have believed me, and he would also have treated me like a Western doll. I didn't ask anything, just wanted to rest here a while. I came here to rest.' She laughed brightly.

All of a sudden I came down with an acute case of indigestion, and the toast and egg that I'd just eaten weighed heavily in my stomach. I felt that the weight that had pressed down upon her life had transferred over and settled onto my own back.

That afternoon, when I was taking my leave, she told me:

'Come back here every weekend and hang out with us. I will always prepare a comfortable bed for you, a sumptuous breakfast, a patio with conversation and laughter, and a welcome heart.'

(The rouge on her lips went right through my shirt and into my skin—my heart was also stained red.)

What a lucky girl!

The trivialities of life are like ants.

One by one the ants line up like number 3s.

Yes! Yes!

There are 333333333333 crawling onto me from all directions without stopping, and I can't get away from them. I'm crushed! I'm really crushed by them! I walk back into life, and as for that white room, the flower garden, the violets hanging in pearl-like chains in front of the patio, the fruity scent of the grape arbour . . . I must throw it all behind me. But one day I'll collapse in the middle of the road!

7 February 1933

Notes

1. A 1928 Hollywood film song.
2. *Strange Tales from a Chinese Studio* (*Liaozhai zhi yi*), by Pu Songling, was an early Qing-dynasty novel about supernatural spirits.
3. A summer resort in western Shanghai.

Index